CONFIGURATION MANAGEMENT

CONFIGURATION MANAGEMENT

The Changing Image

Marion V. Kelly

McGRAW-HILL BOOK COMPANY

London · New York · St Louis · San Francisco · Auckland · Bogotá · Caracas
Lisbon · Madrid · Mexico · Milan · Montreal · New Delhi · Panama · Paris
San Juan · São Paulo · Singapore · Sydney · Tokyo · Toronto

Published by
McGRAW-HILL Book Company Europe
Shoppenhangers Road, Maidenhead, Berkshire, SL6 2QL, England
Telephone 01628 23432
Facsimile 01628 770224

British Library Cataloguing in Publication Data
Kelly, Marion Vilvandre
    Configuration Management: Changing Image
    I. Title
    005.1
    ISBN 0–07–707977–9

Library of Congress Cataloging-in-Publication Data
Kelly, Marion V.
    Configuration management: the changing image/Marion V. Kelly.
        p.   cm.
    Includes bibliographical references and index.
    ISBN 0–07–707977–9 (hardback: alk. paper)
    1. Configuration management.   I. Title.
    QA76.76.C69K45   1996
    005.1'5—dc20   95-43646
                                                                        CIP

McGraw-Hill

A Division of The **McGraw·Hill** Companies

12345 CUP 98765

Typeset by Alden Multimedia, Northampton
and printed and bound in Great Britain at the University Press, Cambridge

Printed on permanent paper
in compliance with ISO Standard 9706

CONTENTS

ACKNOWLEDGEMENTS

I have been very lucky in having a family and set of friends who have supported and encouraged me, in writing this book, well beyond the call of duty! But of all of them, my greatest thanks go to my husband, Mike, who never for a moment doubted my ability—when I certainly did—who gave me invaluable technical advice and constructive criticism, who never complained about the book taking precedence over our social life and made it possible for me to concentrate on trying to be an author instead of a wife and mother, by cooking us wonderful meals! And how can I say thank you enough to our sons, Rupert, Alec and Greg, for their support and for all they have managed to do while I have been glued to my computer?

Thank you, as well, to John Buckle for his inspiration, to Keith Jackson, Judith and Mike Hall, Linda Hall, Jim Hemsley, Ivan Klingels and Tom Thorne for their encouragement over the years, and to my mother, who painstakingly checked the early manuscript for grammatical errors.

I am not sure if I should thank or curse Paul Goodman, because it was he who landed me in this—well aware of the blood, sweat and tears that I would go through, as he had just completed his own book! But I *am* grateful to him—now that it is all over—and my only real regret is that my father (whose own published work awed me so as a child) did not live long enough to see the book published.

TRADEMARKS

Name	*Trademark of*
Macroscope	Objective Incorporated
FrameMaker	Frame Technology Corporation
Software through Pictures	Interactive Development Environments Incorporated
Visio	Shapeware Corporation
WordPerfect	WordPerfect Corporation
Sunos	Sun Microsystems Incorporated
UNIX	AT&T
Yellow Pages	Claritas Incorporated
SCCS	AT&T
RCS	Thompson Automation Software
CMS	Digital Equipment Company
PVCS	Intersolv Corporation
Clearcase	Atria Software Incorporated
CCC/Harvest	Softool Corporation
Workflo	FileNet Incorporated
Documentum	Documentum Incorporated
SmartStream	Dun and Bradstreet Software Services Incorporated
Red Box	Ultracomp
Lotus Notes	Lotus Development Corporation
Lotus Forms	Lotus Development Corporation
LIFESPAN	BAeSEMA Ltd
Continuus	Continuus Software Corporation
CMVision	Expertware Incorporated
PCMS	SQL Software Ltd
VMS	Digital Equipment Company
HP-UX	Hewlett-Packard
Microsoft Windows	Microsoft Corporation

1

UP-FRONT

- YOU, THE READER
- CHAPTERS CONTENTS
- THE APPENDICES

YOU, THE READER

What category of reader do you fall into? Are you someone who has understood the absolute necessity of configuration management (CM) for years and run a good system, despite lack of support from senior management and colleagues, or are you one of the many unfortunates that have suffered from pedantic and ignorant configuration control being forced upon you or your team, causing frustration and delay? Perhaps, you are a frustrated manager who has been trying, unsuccessfully, to gain engineer cooperation in introducing a CM system? Or, maybe, you know little about the subject and are simply dipping into this to see what it is all about and whether or not there is anything in it for you or your project? If you can relate even remotely to any of these, read on.

If, on the other hand, you run or interface to a CM system that:

- is central to your project management;
- enhances technical creativity while keeping careful control of contractual limitations;
- is fully staffed with technically qualified configuration controllers, who are familiar with software and hardware development problems throughout the project life cycle and are willing to and know how to bend the rules on occasion, without jeopardizing the system in any way;
- offers you reliable up-to-date information on any part of the project's configuration (whether software, documentation, drawings, firmware or hardware), but
- never causes unreasonable delay;

then you, alone, can put down this book now, knowing yourself to be a rare and fortunate person!

And that is the crux of it. CM is one of the most essential project management disciplines, which should give customers confidence, support management by supplying reliable contractual, requirement, resourcing and deliverables information and, above all, take the strain off the engineers by allowing them to concentrate on their designs and implementation without worrying about loss of data, corruption of files, illegal access, etc., etc. Yet CM has been ignored and evaded when experienced and far-sighted management have *tried* to impose it, or it has been mismanaged by staff who have no concept of engineering. Sometimes, when a good CM system has been put in place by the many engineers who realize its worth, less well-informed management have not allowed those engineers sufficient time, staff or facilities to do the job as well as they could.

This book has been embarked upon with a feeling of confidence, however, that until recently would have been unfounded. At last, attitudes are changing and the following chapters should supply some of the missing links as to what CM is all about and how it can, and does, help. The approach has been to be as practical as possible, avoiding jargon—or at least explaining it—and relating the various disciplines to all project personnel, in all the conventional phases of development and maintenance project life cycles. There are lots of examples of successes and catastrophes, all of which really happened but, for obvious reasons, the identities of companies, projects and individuals have had to remain anonymous.

CHAPTERS CONTENTS

The title track of this album—Chapter 2—emphasizes the technical aspects of the work involved in CM and shows how attitudes to it are at last changing. It describes the causes of this change, which are both commercial (guided by market changes) and technological (as the hardware and software systems, and the environments on which they are developed, evolve).

The various disciplines of CM are explained at a high level in Chapter 3, which establishes what CM is and why it should be a central part of any information technology (IT) organization and these are then expanded with more practical detail in subsequent chapters.

Chapter 4 puts CM into context *vis à vis* the entire project life cycle. When should a CM system be implemented, how long should it last, and are all the CM disciplines equally relevant to all phases of a project? Must a CM system have been in place from the beginning, or could one be set up halfway through a project, or even only start during its maintenance?

Concentrating on the people involved, **Chapter 5 explains the roles of configuration manager and configuration controller**. The required qualifications and experience for these members of project staff are discussed and a comparison made with what is available in today's market. The physical configuration control department is then described in terms of suitable automation and the requirements for the software and document libraries.

Having established who comprises the CM team, Chapter 6 explores the interfaces to that team and the CM system as a whole. It is not just the engineers or quality assurance (QA) that are involved, but senior management, the customer, commercial and planning departments, and technical authors and secretaries. Obviously, when these interfaces work well the whole system runs smoothly but, where some department falls down, good CM can actually make up for it to a *certain* degree.

Chapters 7 to 10 expand the CM disciplines described in Chapter 3, covering such topics as exactly what does and does not need to be treated as a configuration item (CI). Chapter 7 also introduces 'two-tier control', showing how to beat the 'too much too soon' and 'too little too late' syndromes which baffle so many projects' configuration control. Chapter 8 contains practical advice on how to categorize and structure the CIs, so that there is global understanding of the whole configuration, maximum access efficiency, control of that access, and consideration of CIs being used outside the prime project requirements (all of which results in enormous savings in time and resources). Baselining is covered in Chapter 9, with an explanation of what is meant by this term and advice on how to apply it to save time and resources and to keep project milestones on target. Change control and its inevitable precursor, defect reporting, together with its link to the help desk function are explained in Chapter 10 and the importance of linking the various control forms to the actual CIs they are reporting on is stressed.

Chapter 11 is the 'exception that proves the rule'. Throughout the book the importance of plans and procedures, of rigid control and a totally reliable reporting mechanism is stressed but, as any engineer or project manager knows, there are times when it simply is not possible to follow the rules. This chapter shows how CM should be a help, not a hindrance, and how a good CM system will be able to cope with the impossible delivery deadline, the customer who insists on breaking his own rules, and the engineer who has to release software or distribute a document before it is ready.

'Of the many plagues that afflict humanity—locusts, boils, blackdeath etc.—sudden audits are amongst the most feared', points out Terry Pratchett in one of his 'Discworld' novels, so Chapter 12 shows how to approach audits confidently and attain certification for standards such as ISO 9001 without disruption to normal work, by building in the requisite controls and running constant, painless checks.

Chapter 13 illustrates the sort of information (metrics) that should and should not be collated (measured) on a CM system, and an example measurement programme illustrates the way in which this can be managed to save time and resources, and therefore money, and to ensure continual process improvement.

CM, with its vast quantities of data and repetitive tasks, is an ideal candidate for automation, so Chapter 14 describes the main criteria for the selection of a suitable tool to help this automation, dividing the various tools available into categories, from simple version control to full-blown configuration management. This chapter also provides a shopping list of requirements and a list of questions that should be put to vendors to ensure that the right tool is purchased for the right job.

It is possible that you may reach the Conclusion, in Chapter 15, and still wonder how exactly to set up a CM system! This is deliberate, because the aim has not been to write a textbook which would detail exactly *what* to do but, rather, to explain *why* it should be done. The book is intended as an explanation of current misconceptions and a conversion process for those of you who view the subject with, at best, boredom and, at worst, horror. It is hoped that when you go on to set up and run a CM system, to interface to it or to budget for one, you will do so with a positive, enlightened attitude. Hopefully, by the time those of you who are already running good CM systems reach the Conclusion, you will have been able to consolidate your own ideas and been given the inspiration to continue.

THE APPENDICES

For those of you who read this book because you are looking for suggestions on detailed procedures, the template solutions in Appendix A should be useful. They give examples of career paths and job descriptions, procedures, configuration control forms and reports, as well as practical check lists. They have been called 'template' because they are sufficiently open-ended for you to be able to adapt them for your own project or company, regardless of what phase you are in, what timescales or manpower are involved, or what level of automation is available.

Throughout the book, I have tried to use plain English because, while the computer industry in general is guilty of generating an enormous amount of jargon, CM is perhaps one of the worst culprits. Appendix B, therefore, contains a glossary of terms in which many of the CM 'buzz words' are explained. They should fall into context and no longer baffle or alienate those project members trying to get to grips with what is really an extremely simple, logical and above all practical set of project management disciplines. The glossary also explains the interpretation of various words or phrases as used in this book and lists all of the abbreviations.

The bibliography in Appendix C is, unfortunately, all too short. There are a number of books written on various CM disciplines which contain sound advice and good examples of procedures and configuration control forms. I have read nothing, however—with the possible exception of the Central Computing and Telecommunications Agency (CCTA) IT Infrastructure Library—that looks at the *totality* of the disciplines, relating them to all project personnel and to all phases of projects. Another problem with trying to recommend further reading material is that most books are aimed at the engineer and, while this backs my contention that CM is a technical, not just administrative, function, it is not only the engineer who needs convincing of CM's usefulness, but also often senior management and the customers themselves.

It had been planned, in the proposal for this book, to add a section at this point 'explaining to the reader how the author first became involved in the subject and how projects that she has worked on have benefited, i.e. proof that she practises what she preaches and has seen real results'. Now that the actual book is in front of you, however, you probably would not find a curriculum vitae particularly interesting and, in any case, by the time you have read the whole book, experience in the field will hopefully be self-evident. It is not the author who is important, it is you the reader, and whether or not you can relate to what is written and what could be described as a 'bittersweet involvement' with configuration management!

2

THE CHANGING IMAGE

- WHY CHOOSE CM AS A CAREER?
- JOBS, STANDARDS AND TOOLS
- CONTRACT MARKETS
- ADMINISTRATIVE OR TECHNICAL?
- INDUSTRY ACCEPTANCE
- QUANTUM LEAPS IN CONFIGURATIONS
- SUMMARY

WHY CHOOSE CM AS A CAREER?

There is, at the moment, an almost universal misconception that anyone working in configuration management must be *incapable of* doing anything else.... If you look in the current issue of the British Computer Society's (BCS) 'Industry Structure Model' (ISM), you will find job descriptions and clear career paths for everything from junior programmers to managing directors but you will not find any mention of a configuration controller or configuration manager.

If it is not a proper job, how can we attract the proper people to it? How can we expect engineers with sound technical backgrounds, who have sufficient project management experience and good people-communications skills to branch into what has, certainly until recently, been considered one of the most dead-end and disrespected of roles? The answer is, of course, that few of them will; those who are involved at the moment are either only there by chance or because they understand the importance of CM and are prepared to 'go it alone', often despite lack of acknowledgement or support.

But here is the first change indicator: issue 2 of the ISM may not have considered CM worthy of mention, but proposals for its inclusion in the BCS's new issue, ISM3, were not only accepted, but were demanded impatiently by the team of BCS authors!

Many people wonder why on earth anyone would chose CM as a career. Those people obviously do not realize that it is because CM *can* be exciting and managerially demanding, that it involves work on bids, contracts, development, test and acceptance, delivery and maintenance; that a configuration manager is in constant contact with all levels of project personnel, from the most junior engineer to the project manager and customers (who may be managers from other departments or companies or, perhaps, government ministers!). They do not realize that CM is technically challenging, that while it may be exhausting it is *never* boring and that, above all, the IT industry needs to understand more about CM and to use it properly. Luckily for the industry, more and more technically and managerially competent configuration managers are emerging.

> Once upon a time, there was a junior programmer who thought the data processing manager was God. If only he could know all that, do all that, earn all that! And yet, he had the audacity to harbour niggling doubts that perhaps it wasn't quite right to go to the pub at lunch-time, drink several gin and tonics and then 'enhance' files on the live system. And Mr W always seemed so surprised when the batch run fell over! The programmer did not realize then that his desire to copy the files into some area, safe from the intoxicated dabblings of Mr W, was the seeds of instinctive CM, and it was only years later—when tasked with setting up some form of version control for his team's component—that the words 'configuration control' or 'CM' became part of his vocabulary. From there, however, that engineer moved into CM full-time and became a respected CM consultant, with his own company, having set up and managed several large and successful CM systems.

It is typical of the Law of Cussedness that in all the years I was looking for jobs in configuration control not one was advertised, and that in all the years I wanted to attend seminars to teach me about it there were never any devoted to CM. If it was covered at all, it was only ever as a very minor part of a QA or project management seminar. This is changing too, though, and in the last year there have been advertisements for configuration managers and controllers every week in the computing press. Also, not only are configuration management experts in demand, but the advertisements stress the jobs as being for engineers, not administrators. When I was actively looking for a position as a configuration manager, few agencies even recognized it as a job in its own right and yet, in the last year or so, I have been telephoned numerous times by agencies who cannot find enough people with experience in this field, asking if I know of anyone. Unfortunately, of course, this lack of available experience leaves the field open to the cowboys!

> There was going to be a demonstration of a maintenance tool in a company and the configuration manager let the organizers know

that he would be interested in attending. Five minutes before the start, though, he was surprised to be called out of the demo room by one of the bid managers (who was contemplating using the tool for a maintenance contract he was negotiating) and blusteringly requested not to attend the demo! The configuration manager and the other attendees were absolutely stunned and couldn't think why the man was behaving in this extremely unprofessional way.... It turned out that he had made himself out to be quite an expert on CM in his CV and, for the two years since the configuration manager had joined the company, had lived in terror of being shown up!

Figure 2.1 shows an extract from an article in *DEC Computing* (24 November 1993). A configuration controller stuck a copy of the full article on her office wall, but most

Figure 2.1   Extract from *DEC Computing*

people ignored it. Several nodded in agreement, although one 'clever dick' pointed out that the article did not carry much weight, as it did not say who the experts were!

These reactions typify what is happening in the industry at the moment. Most people do not know much about CM as it simply has not impacted them directly; many people, however, have been running or using CM systems (or, at least, version control systems) for years; but some refuse to find out about it and do not *want* to learn and, because they have never understood what CM is really about, still insist on slamming it and perpetuating its bad press. The same person who criticized the article actually informed the configuration controller authoritatively that 'CM is going out of fashion'—in reality, of course, it is only just coming into fashion!

JOBS, STANDARDS AND TOOLS

But this is also changing, albeit slowly. More people than ever before are learning about CM and starting to see its potential. As already stated, there are now configuration management jobs advertised regularly although, ironically, often the people with the right experience and qualifications to fill them either do not want to or do not realize they could and should do it. There are now seminars dedicated to the subject and, most importantly, there are international standards that have made CM mandatory. In particular, CM is stated as a necessary process in the increasingly popular Capability Maturity Model (CMM) developed by the Software Engineering Institute in Pittsburgh (SEI, 1993). A large proportion of attendees at CM seminars and tools demonstrations nowadays are there because their companies are aiming at ISO 9001 and that means they *have* to have CM.

As companies are forced by standards and competition to prove their CM abilities so they, in turn, will demand the tools with which to do it. Until recently, version control tools were considered perfectly sufficient. But, as the complexity and power of fully integrated CM systems are realized, so much more sophisticated CM tools—as described in Chapter 14—are being developed and existing tools, which have been on the market for years but with little demand, are now being enhanced and ported to more popular platforms at the direct insistence of users.

CONTRACT MARKETS

One of the main catalysts for the increase in awareness of CM is, of course, the change-over from a predominantly costs-plus, to a fixed-price, contract market. Gone are the days of escalating costs being paid for by the hapless customers. Fixed-price contracts and service-level agreements (SLAs) cannot afford rework, must know exactly what impact a new customer requirement will have on the documentation, code, timescales and maintenance costs, and must ensure that what ran smoothly in-house will be guaranteed to work in front of the customer. In other words, *fixed-price contracts cannot afford not to have CM*.

ADMINISTRATIVE OR TECHNICAL?

But, if CM is that important, why is it that so many configuration managers and controllers have never written a line of code or installed a board or laid a cable in their lives and have had little or no project management experience either? The industry seems to have split the disciplines into 'technical' and 'administrative' but then handed all of the latter to staff who cannot relate to the technical parts and vice versa. Of course there are a large number of administrative tasks in CM but, apart from filing and very basic data input, none of the administrative tasks can be done without an eye to the impact on and relationship to the system configuration. Chapter 5 will explain in more detail exactly what the roles of configuration controller and manager entail, but suffice to say that no CM system can be set up, let alone run properly, without sufficient technical knowledge. As the recent advertisements mentioned earlier show, this is also being recognized at last.

One of the most important tasks of a configuration manager is to help the development teams plan their hardware, software and documentation structures, guiding and setting standards across the whole project. This may not have been thought of in the past as a CM function, but who else has the objective interest of the whole project at heart (as opposed to an individual component), coupled with the knowledge of the CM database and requisite experience with whatever CM tool is being used, to know how to get the best performance out of it? Who else is responsible for the control of the configuration (i.e. for all the CI files and structures and their interrelationships, and for all the information relating to them in the CM database) from early project bid stage to final delivery and maintenance, and who else is also involved in releasing the software for build and test, or even for carrying out the requisite builds?

In establishing the CI structures with the respective component team leaders, the configuration manager not only imposes the system standard, but also has the opportunity to learn each component's structural idiosyncrasies and become acquainted with the high-level component and module functions—information that will become essential once these items are submitted to CM. Importantly, too, the configuration manager is established in the eyes of the development teams as someone who understands what they are doing, has 'been there' and, above all, knows what the problems will be during the development life cycle. It is vital to banish the image of 'unsympathetic administrator' right from the start!

INDUSTRY ACCEPTANCE

And, oh, how unsympathetic some can be . . . . So often, when a configuration manager starts a new job, he or she is met with hostility. If that individual is any good, however, that hostility will change to surprised tolerance and, finally, active support and appreciation. 'We thought the CM system would be pretty difficult to live with, but it seems to be able to accommodate whatever problems we pose', said one group manager. It was as if they assumed that the function of a configuration manager was to be as obstructive as possible. The concept of CM being of service to them, of their project management requirements being a prime objective, of being able to create procedures that would help not hinder, and being able to bend those procedures if absolutely necessary, had never occurred to them! This part of the image is, perhaps, one of the first that must change so that managers, not just engineers, welcome rather than tolerate CM.

I say 'not just engineers' because ironically it used to be the development teams that baulked most at the idea of being hobbled by any form of control. But, again there is change, in that software engineering degree courses now cover CM and the youngest engineers are perfectly open to the concept and only wish to know *how* it is done, rather than *why*. Some 'old dogs' though, who are furthest removed from active development of systems, are having difficulty in accepting the changing image of CM and learning the requisite 'new tricks'.

> One 'old dog', who had a configuration manager reporting to him, was a QA manager—which was a mistake from the start, as CM is not a QA responsibility any more than coding is, and should not be part of a QA chain of command. What made it worse was that this QA manager was a hardware QA specialist. He did, in fact, know quite a lot about CM, but refused to acknowledge that there are aspects of *hardware* QA and CM that simply cannot be applied to *software*. 'Don't teach your grandmother to suck eggs' he used to fume when the configuration manager tried to convince him, for instance, that defective software cannot usually be 'segregated' so that it does not 'mix with conforming material' (as required in NATO Standard AQAP-1 para 215) only identified, patched and corrected.

Fortunately, many grandmothers are learning new egg-sucking techniques and the industry is starting to acknowledge that software CM, although very closely related to hardware CM, is not always identical and requires specialist treatment.

QUANTUM LEAPS IN CONFIGURATIONS

And now there is a change in the actual configurations that need to be managed. For many projects the problem is still one of controlling CIs and forms on a single processor or simple network, but more and more companies are having to deal with copies of CIs being held on notebooks and personal organizers. These are sometimes totally isolated but at other times are plugged into a client–server network or even the Internet, with its wonderful potential for information exchange, reuse of code, etc.! The renaissance of the PC has led to a proliferation of new technologies, for example multimedia, corporate and group working, and now the so-called fifth generation languages (5GLs) such as Macroscope (TM), which are revolutionizing the entire software development process to the point where CM might actually be one of the few really necessary project disciplines left! So, does this mean that CM will have to change even before it has really got started? Actually, no, because the beauty of good CM is that it simply does not matter *what* is being controlled (i.e. the CI must be thought of as an *object*)—only that the standard disciplines (described in the next chapter) are stringently applied, albeit with a little lateral thinking!

SUMMARY

So it is not CM, itself, that is changing—only what needs managing and people's perceptions of its value. Proper job descriptions and career paths need to be established in the industry, which will support the growing demand for configuration controllers and managers. Now that there are seminars devoted to CM, more will follow, and the only danger here is of a 'Catch-22' situation in that the new audiences that are attending in order to learn about CM may not have enough experience to ensure that the seminar organizers are not simply 'getting on the bandwagon' with so much humbug. The growing demand for certification to international standards and the trend towards fixed-price contracts will, in turn, produce a growing demand for appropriate automation.

As the tools become more and more capable of fully automating all the disciplines of CM, so their intrinsic technical functionality will further establish the configuration managers and controllers using and customizing them, as engineers not administrators. And, finally, as more technically competent engineers, who know what is needed and why, become involved with configuration management—and apply it to the industry's ever-evolving configurations—so 'job's worth' hindrance should become a thing of the past, together with CM's old and unjustified image.

3

WHAT IS CM
AND WHY?

WHAT?

Figure 3.1 illustrates the four major disciplines of CM which are, unfortunately, often muddled up, misunderstood and misconceived as being complicated. The four disciplines are in fact very straightforward and purely logical ways of ensuring that:

- *you know what you have got to produce;*
- *once you have got it, you know where it is and what state it is in;*
- *only the right people can use or change it and that they will understand the impact of that change;*
- *useful reports are available;*
- *and the agreed procedures are being followed, so that everything hangs together properly.*

That, in a nutshell, is the *raison d'etre* of CM; keep it in mind in the following chapters and test out some of the suggestions made against these criteria.

Figure 3.2 shows how each of the major disciplines is made up of a number of different functions, every one of which is essential to a comprehensive CM system, and is covered in detail in Chapters 7 to 10.

CONFIGURATION IDENTIFICATION

The prime building block of any CM system is configuration identification because, quite simply, if you cannot identify it, you cannot control it! Configuration identification is

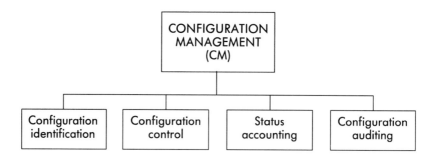

Figure 3.1   The major disciplines of configuration management

CM's *planning function*, establishing up-front, albeit at a high level, what will be needed for the total configuration. This includes planning the structures for all the system's configuration items (CI)s and their interrelationships and planning naming conventions for the actual CIs, their files, the versions of those files, and the issue or release names or numbers.

It involves planning when the baselines will occur, and allocating mnemonics to each CI and build. Finally, it means planning a numbering system for all the control forms (i.e. defect reports, change requests, etc.) affecting them. For maintenance projects, the luxury of planning is often unavailable and configuration identification takes on more of a 'What has been thrown over the wall?' aspect—in other words, reverse engineering. But the need to identify CIs, structures, files, baselines, forms, etc., is just as relevant for a maintenance as for a green field development project, even if— or in fact because—in both cases the plans will need to be modified as the project life cycle progresses.

As each CI is identified and developed, it becomes necessary to safeguard it from corruption while, at the same time, making it widely available for use and enhancement. This is configuration control—the second CM building block and it breaks down into three sub-disciplines: the controlled area or library, problem (or defect) reporting and change control.

CONFIGURATION CONTROL
CONTROLLED AREA/LIBRARY
None of the configuration identification functions would make much sense if there were no controlled area or library in which to store the CIs. As with any high street library, some mechanism has to be established for logging the items, or submitting them, so that it is clear exactly what items the library contains. But that is not actually enough for a CM library because CIs usually have lots of different versions, all of which

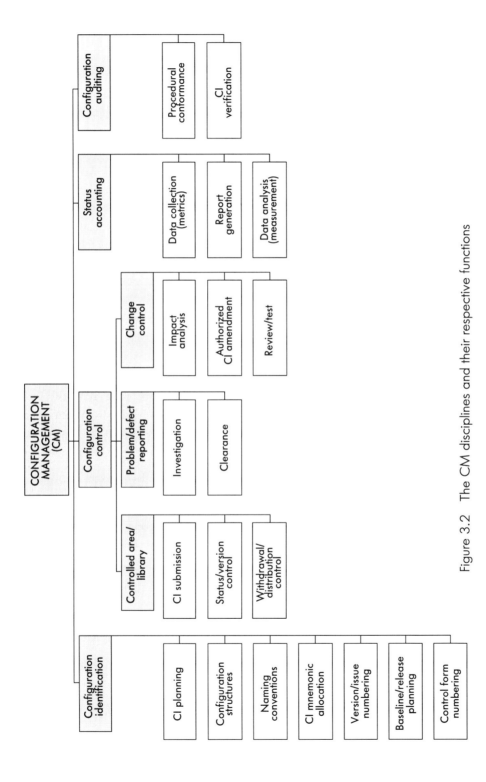

Figure 3.2   The CM disciplines and their respective functions

need identifying and storing. So, the controlled area/library offers a safe repository for all the versions of all the CIs. Unless someone is going to use them, however, this is a fairly pointless exercise, so the final controlled area/library function is to ensure that the 'right' people—and only the 'right' people—can access the 'right' versions of the 'right' CIs easily, to browse or use them, or to investigate and/or change them if they need enhancing or something is found to be wrong with them.

PROBLEM/DEFECT REPORTING

If something is wrong with a CI, there needs to be a mechanism for reporting it, and this is the link between the controlled area/library and the second of the configuration control functions, problem/defect reporting. It is not sufficient just to identify a problem; the discipline must encompass the investigation of that problem and its satisfactory clearance. A problem (or defect) report may, of course, simply be cancelled if, for example, the reporter used an incorrect key sequence. More often, however, defect clearance requires either the creation of a new CI (which links back to configuration identification, since there will be an addition to the structures or files) or, most frequently, some form of change to the existing CI(s) in the controlled area.

CHANGE CONTROL

Changes must not be allowed, though, unless they are controlled. Look at the first box under the change control heading in Figure 3.2. So often, changes that have been made to a CI are carefully documented but the *impact* of the change on the CI (and those associated with it in the total configuration) has never been properly analysed. What appeared to be a controlled change actually results in chaos. Only after thorough impact analysis—both technical (i.e. 'what CIs are affected?') and resources/timescales (i.e. 'how many people, at what grade, will be needed to effect this change and for how long?')—has taken place should a CI be updated. Part of that update is then to ensure that the changed CIs are thoroughly re-reviewed or re-tested, to make sure that the approved change, the whole approved change and nothing but the approved change has been correctly implemented.

> For example, sometime between the late bid stage of Project A and its final acceptance, one small word crept into the contract; the original draft contract had defined part of a deliverable as:
>
> '. . . helicopter launching pad . . .'
>
> The version of the contract to which the customer insisted on compliancy read:
>
> '. . . helicopter *and* launching pad . . .'!

Because the contract was not under configuration control, nobody knew when the word had appeared or who had inserted it or even whether it had been deliberate or simply a typing error; whatever the cause, it cost the contractor a small fortune!

Configuration control could either have avoided this catastrophe altogether or, at least, radically reduced its impact.

STATUS ACCOUNTING

The processes of identification, CI submission and control, defect reporting and change control described above can generate large quantities of data, even on the smallest of projects. Unless that data is analysed and acted upon, however, it is pointless. Status accounting—the next major CM building block or discipline—is, therefore, the collection of information and the generation of reports, coupled with their analysis. In the story of the helicopter launching pad, status accounting should have been able to prove (by interrogating a change request database and producing relevant reports) that the 'and' in question had never been intended nor had been approved by either contractor or customer, thus saving the contractor from having to foot the bill.

CONFIGURATION AUDITING

Finally, because CM is useless unless it can be totally relied upon, it is necessary to ensure that all the agreed procedures are carried out to make it work properly and, also, to verify that the information about the CIs and their structures, supplied through status accounting, is correct. This constitutes the last major CM discipline, configuration auditing, and it is the one that often seems the least interesting (or even least important). But it is—like all of the disciplines—essential. In the helicopter story, it should have been possible to follow an audit trail to show how and when the error had crept in so that, at the very least, such a costly mistake would never happen again; in other words to effect process improvement.

WHY?

The answer to the question 'What is configuration management?', then, is that it is a set of highly proceduralized and interrelated project management disciplines which identify, control and document all of a project's configuration. As to 'Why?', the main reason for implementing a sound CM system is not, contrary to common belief, to hamper engineers or to prevent some old administrator from being made redundant but is, quite simply, *to save time and money*. For example, experience has shown that it costs approximately ten times more to correct an item once it has been delivered, than it does while it is being coded, so that the high or low cost in terms of manpower and time of any warranty or maintenance programme is directly affected by the high or low quality of the project's configuration management system!

SUMMARY

It is obvious that any items will be more easily traceable and usable if unambiguously identified and, once an item works, it makes sense to put it in a 'safe deposit' or library (not in terms of dropping it into a black hole, but for reliable access). The better the CM system's defect reporting procedures, the fewer times a defect will have to be investigated and, with comprehensive change control, changes will be straightforward to analyse and can be implemented with known technical/time/cost impact, instead of hidden ones.

So that everyone—from the most junior engineer to the customer—knows what is going on, status accounting will ensure that accurate reports are available and, finally, configuration auditing will check that all those involved are following the agreed procedures and that the system (and every part of it—whether software files, hardware installations, drawings or documentation) really is what it is believed to be.

Remember, the CM disciplines are just sensible routines for ensuring that:

- *you know what you have got to produce;*
- *once you have got it, you know where it is and what state it is in;*
- *only the right people can use or change it and that they will understand the impact of that change;*
- *useful reports are available;*
- *and the agreed procedures are being followed properly.*

4

WHERE DOES CM BELONG IN A PROJECT?

- PROJECT PHASES
- RELEVANT CM DISCIPLINES
- THE PROJECT TEAMS INVOLVED
- INTRODUCING CM ANYWHERE, ANYTIME
- 'QUICK FIXES' v. CONFIGURATION CONTROL
- SUMMARY

PROJECT PHASES

CM is *not* a function that should be instigated once there are some documents, software or hardware installations that need controlling, and phased out once delivery has taken place. Sometimes it may not be possible to implement CM before this (and mid-project and maintenance introduction of CM is dealt with later) but, ideally, a project should take advantage of at least some aspects of CM from its bid stage, right through until the end of the project life cycle (i.e. after warranty/maintenance).

RELEVANT CM DISCIPLINES

But, if all the phases are subject to CM, are *all* its disciplines relevant to each phase? No—this would be overkill and would hinder rather than help. During the bid stage, for example, once the contract looks to be a 'pretty fair bet', the main bid documentation should be submitted to the configuration library, because it is from this that the contract will emerge. Even if the contract is never awarded, this material or parts of it will in all likelihood prove useful for other bids and should not risk being mislaid or corrupted. Many projects have had to cope with totally unnecessary problems caused by unsolicited changes, which make it differ from what was agreed during the pre-contract negotiations, being introduced to a final contract (remember the helicopter story!).

Figure 4.1 illustrates the relative impact of the various CM disciplines to each project phase. Configuration identification would be relevant at the bid stage, because there are likely to be other bids, so the new one needs to be uniquely identified. (This may

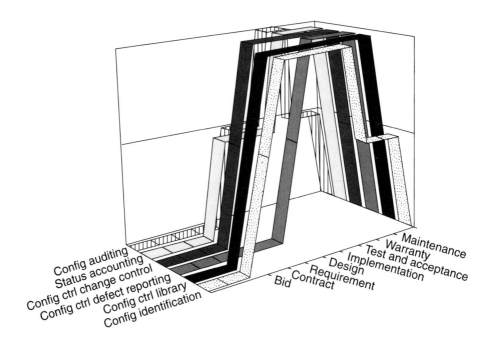

Figure 4.1   The relative applicability of CM disciplines to project phases

seem obvious, but one company had four different documents, each with the title 'Secure Communications Specification', for four entirely unrelated bids and they got horribly mixed up!)

It may also be necessary to apply access control to ensure, for example, that sub-contractors working on another project cannot view the new bid material. Version control would also be needed so that differences in versions can be tracked, but defect reporting and full change control would be redundant. Status accounting and auditing (apart from at a general, company level) would also be superfluous, *unless* the new bid team needed to know what was available for use from another project and what state it was in.

Full CM really only comes into play, then, following contract award, with the contract itself being the first fully controlled CI. Early on, during the requirements and design phases, there may be a few defects reported on these high-level documents but, on the whole, defect reporting only emerges as a major discipline once low-level design and implementation are well under way and then of course, continues into warranty and maintenance. Change control, on the other hand, will have been active from the moment the contract was signed, with an accent on customer-impact changes (i.e. to the contract itself and the requirements or procurement documents), and this is just as relevant to enhancements to maintenance contracts, particularly where service level agreements (SLAs) are in force.

Once design and development start, the accent will move to internal, rather than customer, changes to CIs such as design and test documentation, the application software and the hardware and proprietary software environment. Status accounting and audits obviously play a part throughout, but implementation is the stage at which these two disciplines prove really helpful. They enable test engineers to track what defects have and have not been cleared in a particular build; they help development engineers check which changes were implemented in which versions of files or complete components; and they enable QA and project management to keep a 'weather eye' on trends, through analysis (measurement) of data (metrics) produced from the CM controlled area/library.

THE PROJECT TEAMS INVOLVED

Just as different phases of the project place emphasis on the different CM disciplines, so the various phases involve varying sections of the project team. Figure 4.2 lists the project phases and plots against them a list of the sections of personnel involved in a typical development project, with an indication of where each of those sections is

Function/Phase	Bid	Contract	Requirements	Design	Implementation	Acceptance	Warranty	Maintenance
Customer	✓	✓	✓			✓	✓	✓
Quality assurance	✓	✓	✓	✓	✓	✓	✓	✓
Configuration management	✓	✓	✓	✓	✓	✓	✓	✓
Project management	✓	✓	✓			✓		✓
Development team leaders		✓	✓	✓	✓	✓	✓	✓
Engineers				✓	✓		✓	✓
Acceptance test engineers		✓	✓			✓	✓	✓
System support (development environment)				✓	✓	✓	✓	✓
Technical documentation	✓	✓	✓			✓		✓

Figure 4.2   Project phases and respective function involvement

most active. Although a development project life cycle has been illustrated, virtually the same phases and personnel apply to a maintenance project:

- The *customer* and senior *project management* are, obviously, closely involved with the bid, contract, requirements and acceptance documents, but they are unlikely to impact design and implementation, which are the domain of the *development team leaders* and their *engineers*.
- *Acceptance test engineers* will, of course, be involved with both contract and acceptance, since it is they who will need to demonstrate that the delivered system answers its requirements but, like the customer and project management, their involvement in design and implementation is slight.
- *System support* (or environment bureau) will not really impact the project until the design phase (although they may have been responsible for the environment which supported production of the bid, contract and requirements documents) but, from that point on, system support will obviously be vital, supplying and maintaining the hardware and software environment on which the project will be developed and tested and from which it will be delivered and, possibly, maintained.
- The *technical documentation team* or, where this function does not exist, the secretaries, will be involved spasmodically throughout the project, producing deliverable documentation such as the contract and any sub-contracts, the requirements or procurement specifications and test certification and, perhaps, technical authorship of user documentation.

Figure 4.3 highlights two interesting facts from the original table. First, with the exception of QA—which should by its very nature oversee every aspect of a project—CM is the only function that is actively involved in every phase of the project life cycle. Second, the only phase of the project which involves (or at least *should* involve) all sections of personnel is maintenance. Here lies one of the major sources of potential catastrophe because, inevitably, by the time maintenance comes along, either the whole system is 'thrown over the wall' to an entirely separate department or even organization or, even if it is the same department, most of the staff will have been moved on to other projects! So, the information held in the central CM system is the single continuous strand which can link the new, often part-time, maintenance staff, to the original development. It is necessary, therefore, to:

Think of CM as a spinal cord, linking all parts of the nervous system; it provides the single channel through which all information can flow, but protects it with hard and yet flexible vertebrae!

Function/Phases	Bid	Contract	Requirements	Design	Implementation	Acceptance	Warranty	Maintenance
Customer	✓	✓	✓			✓	✓	✓
Quality assurance	✓	✓	✓	✓	✓	✓	✓	✓
Configuration management	✓	✓	✓	✓	✓	✓	✓	✓
Project management	✓	✓	✓			✓		✓
Development team leaders			✓	✓	✓	✓	✓	✓
Engineers				✓	✓		✓	✓
Acceptance test engineers		✓	✓			✓	✓	✓
System support (development environment)				✓	✓	✓	✓	✓
Technical documentation	✓	✓	✓			✓		✓

Figure 4.3   CM—the continuity factor in the project life cycle

INTRODUCING CM ANYWHERE, ANYTIME

Ideally, the relevant CM disciplines should be implemented through all project phases and involve all project personnel. This approach will result in a technical, administrative and commercial core, far removed from the peripheral 'tag on' (or wart!) mistakenly implemented by many projects. However, it is also important to allow for the introduction of CM anywhere, anytime. Chapter 3 pointed out that if you cannot identify it, you cannot hope to control it and this is the single most important factor in introducing a CM system at any stage in a project.

> For example, the company Transfer of Knowledge (TOK) Ltd were involved in a quality improvement programme (QIP) for a section of the Dutch Department of Social Security, 'GAK'. Their CM consultant was tasked with assessing how this client could introduce CM, integrating it into current working practices in line with the QIP disciplines that were being simultaneously introduced, to attain ISO 9001 certification. What was interesting about this consultancy task was that the 200-man section of GAK to which the consultant was assigned dealt with nothing but maintenance. All the design and development work was the responsibility of other GAK sections which would not come under the same QIP umbrella for some time. Because the sections were totally independent, there was little or no

communication between them; there were varying degrees of documentation which accompanied the various systems to be maintained, but nothing resembling a controlled configuration. In some cases, all that had been received 'over the wall' was a single tape, without even a directory listing, let alone any form of file versioning or design information.

Obviously it would not be possible to put all the Dutch social security systems under full configuration management in one fell swoop; it would be essential not to disrupt the current work, while proving to the maintenance teams that what the consultant was preaching would really help them in practice. Starting slowly and modestly, they took one relatively small system as a prototype and the first task for that system team leader was to make his best guess at what the configuration comprised. The consultant tasked the team leader to produce a system specification tree (SST) (see Appendix B and Chapter 8 for a detailed explanation) so, using very simple reverse engineering, they established that the system consisted of five major components.

Then, because three of those components had had problems which the team had already had to work out and resolve, they were able to add module and file details to those component structures, defining component and module identities and allocating a version '1' to all files, to establish the first baseline. This left two components with nothing more than a high-level node name. If, subsequently, there were never any defects reported or enhancements required on these nodes, then the lower-level information would never be needed; if, on the other hand, they ever did require changing, then the missing lower-level information could be filled in then.

The pilot scheme software was placed in a controlled area, and defect reporting and change control introduced on those nodes that had been identified. Using registers (see Appendices A.6, A.7 and A.8) on the control forms and build state logs (see Appendix B) to show what versions of files were changed, together with a master configuration index (see Chapter 9 and Appendix A.5) to log what little documentation existed at that stage, the pilot system had all it needed to run effectively. It could now start saving large amounts of time, because all the team knew what the system consisted of, how most of it interrelated, where to go for further information and, over the following months, could easily fill in the missing links as they were required.

So, CM can start halfway through or even virtually at the end of a project, the important thing being to establish exactly what and where everything is at a chosen point in time. That configuration knowledge can then slowly be added to with each defect that is cleared or each enhancement that is introduced, until a complete re-engineered picture can be drawn in the form of an SST. All the known system CIs can be safely controlled in a library—as if full configuration control had been in place from the original requirement—and other records in the form of build state logs, test reports, control form registers, etc. can be built up.

'QUICK FIXES' v. CONFIGURATION CONTROL

It is worth spending a little time on defect reporting and change control in warranty and maintenance specifically, as there is often a total misconception that 'quick fixes' and configuration control are contradictions in terms. Of course software in the field has to be 'patched'; if the cash dispenser at a bank or a family allowance payment were unavailable for weeks (because the defect reports on the software had not been filled in correctly, the main signatory on the change requests was on holiday, the test and acceptance environment could not be set up until next week because another version of the operating system had been installed to test another system, the configuration control board was not due to meet until the end of the month, etc., etc.) all hell would break loose!

All live systems (with the *possible* exception of safety-critical systems) have to have a mechanism in place whereby a knowledgeable engineer can install some form of 'patch' to keep the system running. What is essential, however, is that the engineer completes a defect report at the *same time* as the patch is installed (not at the end of the week!) giving full and exact details of what files have been altered in any way and *how*. In background mode the defect report can then be carefully analysed to see what else might be affected, and decisions taken as to whether the formal clearance of the problem should be exactly as carried out by the engineer on-site or whether, perhaps, it would be better to introduce an already planned enhancement which would remove the necessity for that particular piece of software to be used, etc. Obviously, the better the CM system that has controlled the software throughout its development, the easier and quicker it will be to make such decisions, because information should be immediately to hand on such things as whether or not similar defects have been reported before and if so, when and how were they cleared. The point is that, so long as a working 'patch' is in place, there is time to look at all the defects to be cleared and the enhancements planned for that particular component or system and to decide what should be done and how and, in terms of delivery baselines, when. The 'patch', therefore, remains valid until the next delivery when it will be completely overwritten with the fully analysed, upgraded, tested and controlled software.

SUMMARY

To summarize this chapter, then, a CM system might not actually be introduced on a project by its development teams at all, but by those responsible for its maintenance—which means it might be the customer, not the original development contractor! Ideally, some form of CM should be set in place at final bid stage and should *escalate* through the project both in terms of phases and the people involved, fitting in to whatever is needed, without overkill. The way to avoid this overkill is to ensure that only the *relevant* CM disciplines are used for each of the project phases and to involve the project teams, appropriately.

If it is not possible to set up a CM system at the start of a project it can still be achieved later on, by first identifying where a project has got to and what items it consists of and then, slowly but surely, bringing those items under control—not in some 'big bang' exercise, but as and when each item or hierarchy of items, needs further development.

Regardless of when CM is introduced, it should always be in operation at the end since the customer/user acceptance certificates are possibly the most important configuration items of all! 'I had always thought that the test and acceptance team would be the last ones involved,' said a project manager recently, 'but I realize now that it will be the configuration manager who actually turns out the lights.' Remember to:

---

think of CM as a spinal cord, linking all parts of the nervous system; it provides the single channel through which all information can flow, but protects it with hard and yet flexible vertebrae!

5

THE CM TEAM
AND LIBRARY

- RECRUITMENT PROBLEMS
- CM TEAM ORGANIZATION
- FACILITIES REQUIRED
- THE CONTROLLED AREA
- CONFIGURATION CONTROL FORMS
- SUMMARY

RECRUITMENT PROBLEMS

As no CM system could possibly succeed without the right people setting it up and running it, Appendix A contains a draft interpretation of what the British Computer Society (BCS) might have included in the second issue of their 'Industry Structure Model' (ISM2) to define career paths and job descriptions for configuration managers or controllers. As mentioned in Chapter 2, ISM3 is due to be published at approximately the same time as this book and it will detail the roles and tasks that make up the CM function, showing how a candidate can move through the respective levels of experience and recommending appropriate training and academic achievements for each.

If you read through the descriptions of the models in Appendix A, you will see that CM offers a clear career path from graduate intake level, or equivalent, to very senior management. For those not familiar with the BCS models, they fall into 10 'levels', where level 0 is an inexperienced undergraduate or equivalent, and level 9 is a directorate. Ideally, a configuration controller would enter the CM career path at about level 3, having worked for a number of years as a software or hardware engineer, having gained some experience in team leadership and task planning, and being familiar with the project life cycle and the problems facing engineers at each phase. Configuration managers should be level 5 or above, and move from small projects to large ones, to the configuration management of total companies, as well as to consultancy.

> One company needed to recruit a configuration controller and
> advertised in the standard computing journals. Although they were

disappointed with the low number of responses (given that at that time—1993—there was rampant unemployment, and redundancy figures in the IT industry were rising every day), there were several curriculum vitae (CVs) that sounded interesting. When they started interviewing, however, they found the most appalling mismatch in what many of the CVs said and what the candidates could actually do. It was not so much that they were lying or even exaggerating in their CVs, but that the terminology for CM is so full of jargon and the job descriptions so lacking in standardization that what sounded quite reasonable on paper, turned out more often than not to be absolutely hopeless. For example, one applicant had described himself as:

'A technical administrator, experienced in CM at a senior level. Having a mature and professional approach to colleagues, customers and suppliers. Experienced in training and developing staff ... with a sound knowledge of computer systems ... methodical and analytical approach to problem solving ...'

This sounded just what the company was looking for but, when asked to explain more about how he had been controlling the software (after he had talked himself to a standstill on document control), he replied blithely 'Well, you know what software engineers are like—I was, of course, responsible for software control but I found it best just to leave them to their own devices really.' What is so wonderful about this response is that the candidate actually believed he *was* in control and that, software engineers being the irresponsible hackers he obviously believed them all to be, no one could be expected to do anything else but accept whatever code they gave him! He had no concept of what software engineering involved or of what the engineers' problems might be and, in addition, was obviously totally lacking the inter-personal skills to impose any form of procedural control, to help them or the project.

Another applicant's CV listed her duties for a 'Change Control Engineer' as including:

'The configuration and change control of engineering documentation using both manual and computerized database facilities, carrying out "where used" checks and maintaining compatibility of product family trees for both hardware and software ...'

Looking back at the interview assessment for this lady, the interviewer has written 'Although called a Change Control Engineer, she is one of those that have given the job a bad name. She has done nothing but mindless paper pushing and is not keen on having to work too hard'! When asked exactly what she did to 'maintain compatibility of product family trees' or 'carry out where used checks', she had answered confidently 'Well if I was asked to update the family tree I'd pin up whatever bits of paper they gave me'!

Until the IT Industry can firm up on just what experience and qualifications a configuration controller must have and how these can be developed to offer a demanding, recognized and remunerative career, 'job's-worths' like those described will continue to masquerade as configuration controllers. Frighteningly, many will succeed in getting the jobs, simply because there are so few who apply for the positions, and because those doing the interviewing are often not quite sure what they really want—again because, with the exception of the CCTA's IT Infrastructure Library (ITIL) Service Support Set CM Module (CCTA, 1990), there are no industry guidelines. The ITIL Module sums up the recruitment problem for the CM team as follows:

> It is sometimes difficult to recruit and retain staff with the requisite skills because the work can be perceived as less interesting or creative than, for example, applications development. Potential recruits should be advised that the Configuration Management Group occupies a pivotal role within IT services and offers exposure to, and opportunities to learn from, staff in many other IT groups.

Obviously others have identified a need for an image change, too!

CM TEAM ORGANIZATION

How many configuration managers and controllers do you actually need? Even the smallest of projects will require one of each because *someone* has got to have responsibility for designing the CM system, writing the CM plan and procedures and checking that the system works correctly throughout the project. Someone must also do or oversee the actual submissions of CIs, control and maintain the CM database, progress the change requests, etc. 'What, even on a tiny project?' you cry in horror! Yes—but they do not have to be full-time jobs; either or both could be done by the *same person* who might also have a technical authority role in the project or be a test and acceptance engineer, for example. The point is that the work of establishing exactly what level of CM is appropriate for a particular project and how the various CM disciplines will be

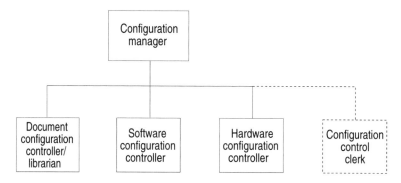

Figure 5.1   The CM team structure for a large project

run and when, *must be formally carried out*. No matter how small a project is there must, by definition, be at least one deliverable and that deliverable, again by definition, must be a CI. So there must be some level of CM, assessed and implemented by someone with the appropriate experience and qualifications.

Figure 5.1 illustrates the ideal structure for a CM team for a large project (or for a CM system spanning several small to medium projects). You can see that the configuration controllers have been categorized into 'document', 'software' and 'hardware'. This is because, although all should be able to handle a large part of each other's work (in terms of CI control, database update, report generation, etc.) and, of course, have an overall understanding of the total CM system, they should come from different backgrounds and have differing specialist knowledge. Thus, the software configuration controller should have spent several years in a programming environment and be able to relate not only to software engineering problems, but also be able to take on the actual building of components, using the requisite compilers and project-specific scripts, if required. Likewise, the hardware configuration controller should be able to understand and advise on the CI structures for, say, a wide area network (WAN) between sites, each with a local area network (LAN) connecting the various offices and processors, printers, etc., within them. The role of document configuration controller becomes evident later in this chapter, in the section on the document library. The configuration control clerk's role is simply that of data input and filing, so that the more expensive configuration controller resources are not wasted.

The configuration manager will be responsible for planning, setting up and managing the CM system and team, supplying advice on CM tools and system applicability for bids and giving potential clients confidence (as detailed in Appendix A.1). The configuration manager will, inevitably, have a large number of potential contract or

SLA changes to investigate and manage, all of which might impact any part of the overall system configuration. Since the configuration manager may also be responsible for more than one project configuration he/she will need to ensure that, where possible, software is reusable and that documentation templates and hardware configuration information is available for *new* contracts to build on. To do all this, a configuration manager should have worked as a configuration controller for several years and, before that, have been a software or hardware engineer, adding project management skills to this through appropriate training and/or experience.

There is a section devoted to 'People' in the CCTA's ITIL CM Module, which sums up what has been said, as follows:

> The success of implementation depends on having enough trained staff. If the Configuration Management Group is understaffed or staffed by people who have not been adequately trained, it could become a bottleneck. Understaffing can also lead to critical errors which could cost more to put right than the cost of adequate staffing in the first place. Additional staff may be required for a short period at implementation time (e.g. to assist with the CI inventory and/or populating the CMDB). Configuration Management is important work which requires staff who will adopt a painstaking approach and pay due attention to detail.

FACILITIES REQUIRED

So, except on the very smallest of projects, there should be a team consisting of a configuration manager and one or more configuration controllers and a data input/filing clerk. Unfortunately, the amount of office space and the computer facilities required by such a team is disproportionate to their numbers because, as already stated, their job is to control not only all versions of all the software, hardware and drawings, but all issues of all document CIs as well, to be able to report on those CIs with up-to-the-minute information, and to make the CIs available to the right people at the right time throughout the project.

The CM team and the controlled area/library have got to be located centrally to the project, for a start. No engineers are going to walk up two flights of stairs to get a controlled document, if they can take an illegal copy of one in the next-door office. If it takes two days to extract a build of software, a set of soft copy hardware inventories or an 'As Built' set of drawings from the controlled area, then is it surprising that the engineers use the easily accessible, but uncontrolled, versions in their own directories instead?

Another physical requirement for a CM area is wallspace. Chapter 8 explains how to plan the CI structures and describes what is known as the system specification tree (SST). Even on a small project the print-out or 'handrolic' drawing of these structures will take up a lot of space and it is no good folding the diagrams away in a drawer or listing folder. They have to be immediately to hand, on a wall, where the CM team and all other project personnel can immediately find the structural location and issue status of a particular CI and see to what overall builds or baselines it relates.

THE CONTROLLED AREA

This is the term for any part of the logical CM system that contains a CI, in any format. The physical controlled area—or CM library as it is sometimes called—is actually made up of several parts. *Soft* copy (i.e. electronic) CIs are held in an electronic library—the logical vault or database for which may be spread over a number of platforms and include a fire safe for tapes and diskettes. *Hard* copy (i.e. paper) CIs are held in a document library—which may consist of a lockable room, filing cabinets and/or cupboards.

It is not essential to purchase a CM tool to support the controlled area, but it *is* essential to have the main facilities listed in Chapter 14. For small and uncomplex projects, these facilities could be provided by using paper control forms and manual registers, by segregating soft files into different directories or even on to separate processors, by writing scripts that will interrogate a small database, etc. But beware—it is easy to fall into the trap of spending a lot of time and therefore money on 'DIY' CM, that often never quite does the job or only works if a particular engineer is running it! It will often cost *less*, in real terms, to buy a minimum-user licence for a proper tool that will automate all the CM disciplines, as well as providing a modicum of training in CM and use of the tool. Chapter 14 goes into great detail about the various requirements for CM automation and needs to be read carefully before any tool is purchased.

THE ELECTRONIC LIBRARY

The electronic library holds the soft copies of all the CIs and, preferably, the electronic configuration control forms as well. It has to be accessible to all project members so, where more than one processor is involved they should, ideally, be networked. This is not essential, in that files can be copied to tape or disc and transported between systems, but this is time-consuming, prone to corruption and can be very expensive on tapes! As with all parts of the controlled area, the electronic library has to be very carefully protected; it should be possible to apply different levels of electronic access control so that, for instance, everyone on the project can *read* files (whether belonging to the CIs themselves, or the control forms affecting them), but only the engineer responsible for their creation and his/her team leader should be allowed to *change* them.

There must be allowance for fire protection too, although responsibility for this will probably be shared with system support. Whether CI tapes/discs are held in a fire safe or in another building, they are still part of the controlled area, and access control to them must be as stringent as to those files residing on the CM processor or in hard copy filing cabinets.

Disc space was mentioned earlier, as being something that has to be budgeted for when setting up a CM system. This is the most underestimated commodity of all, and one that causes problems on most projects. For a start, it is often difficult to estimate how much space a deliverable application is likely to take up. But whatever that figure is, you then have to budget space for half a dozen versions of the entire system; *plus* all its test programs and data; for several versions of all the documentation associated with it; and for the database of control forms (unless these are paper only). This is the minimum because of course, if you run a duplicate development control system, as recommended in Chapter 7, then there may be 20 or even 30 versions of everything!

> The CM system for one of the sub-contractors of a large office communications project used the same CM tool as its customer, the prime contractor, and so the sub-contractor's configuration manager used to discuss the tool's bugs and features with the customer's project manager, Mr B. About halfway through the project, both the sub-contractors and the customer started running low on disc space for their respective CM systems. One afternoon, Mr B came into the configuration manager's office saying he had solved their space problem and had heard that the sub-contractors had solved their problem too. The configuration manager confirmed that they had installed a second disc and spread the configuration over more partitions. 'Ah,' said Mr B, rubbing the side of his nose in a thoughtful manner, 'you solved it *that* way, did you?' This caught the configuration manager on the hop as, try as he might, he could not envisage any other way of coping with his disc space problem and he was intrigued to know what Mr B had done .... 'We've reverted to a *manual* system,' Mr B announced gravely!

Obviously this story has its funny side, but the appalling truth is that the sub-contractors were running a relatively sophisticated, automated CM system which, being for only one sub-contract, was a fraction of the size or complexity of the full system; there was no way that they could have managed manually, so how on earth could Mr B? The answer, of course, is that Mr B *did not* manage—the prime contractor's configuration was a mess and Mr B literally had to depend on the sub-contractor's CM information to make some sort of sense out of the full, integrated system! So beware, try to estimate disc space requirements for the CM system and all its CIs as accurately as possible, and then ensure that the hardware platform is upgradable, in case you have underestimated.

THE DOCUMENT LENDING LIBRARY

This part of the CM system should operate just like any high-street lending and reference library, except that all back-issues of the CI documents should be available for reference as well (albeit clearly marked 'archived' so that there is no confusion as to what is the latest issue). With each lending copy of a document, there should also be the loose-leaf 'master' for (re)distribution and copying and, ideally, some form of 'keyword' search should be available, so that borrowers can browse the library entries by subject, not just title. Unlike a high-street library, allowance has to be made for borrowers leaving an organization, and a mechanism put in place to ensure that all hard copy CIs on loan are returned to the library.

This part of CM might be labelled a purely administrative function, but much time and effort can be saved if the librarian has an in-depth knowledge of the documents available and their relationship to other CIs; of how they or other documents or the software or hardware relating to them might be changing; what contractual implications, if any, there are; how best to use the CM tool(s) to extract relevant information, etc. The function must be run by a properly trained and experienced configuration controller although, as already mentioned, the data input and filing tasks should be delegated.

There should be a straightforward procedure for submitting the soft and hard copies of the documents, linking them to their agreed places in the configuration structure (see Chapter 8) and for reporting on what is available for loan, at what issue, and which copy number of a document has been loaned/distributed to whom. Copy numbers are needed, by the way, to ensure that updates are correctly distributed and that out-of-date issues are destroyed. The exact location of each hard copy document (whether spiral bound, loose leaf, hardback, etc.) should be easily traceable, with a mechanism put in place for logging what has been borrowed, when and by whom, and when returned.

In security-sensitive projects, it may be necessary to have some form of authorization for a loan and, of course, all the documents will have to be under lock and key because that is the only way borrowing can be controlled. Where there is a policy of open 'browse' access to electronic copies of documents, these should always include the text 'Uncontrolled, unless signed and/or numbered' at the top of the document, in case they are printed out. While on the subject of electronic copies, it is tempting to think that the 'electronic office' can do away with all paper documents. Research has shown that comprehension of anything on a screen is only 30 per cent as accurate as of anything printed, however, so the necessity for a hard copy document library will probably continue for some time.

A PROJECT REFERENCE LIBRARY

An obvious extension to the CI document library is a project reference library for proprietary/packaged manuals, user guides and industry journals, etc. These should not be treated as CIs, but can be logged as library items (LIs) and then stored, lent and managed by the document configuration control function with similar, but less stringent, physical and electronic controls.

CONFIGURATION CONTROL FORMS

It is obvious that all sorts of controls are needed to run the above functions smoothly and, to effect these controls, information (such as 'who has permission to change this software?', 'what documents does A. Nichols have out on loan?', etc.) is going to have to be made available. The ideal data collection mechanism is a form and so the controlled area needs submission (or CI record) and withdrawal (or loan) forms. Appendices A.2 and A.3 list the requisite fields for submission and withdrawal forms which could be used for both electronic and hard copy libraries, together with field-by-field explanations as to respective purposes and responsibilities. Figure 5.2 shows how these two forms, together with defect reports and change requests, should be used to control the CI life cycle, through development and testing to delivery and warranty/maintenance.

These forms could be paper only with manual logs, paper logged in a computer-ized database, or electronic only, depending on the size and complexity of the project. If paper only, then the forms should be filed in CI order, to facilitate manual access. If part or wholly electronic, then facilities should be made available for interrogating the forms database on whatever search and/or sort criteria are required. For example, it should be easy to report on such information as 'All incidents or defects associated with one particular CI', or to identify 'All CIs to be delivered by a sub-contractor and their current state of submission'. As can be seen from these two examples, few projects can afford *not* to have some form of CM database to provide this sort of powerful and widely usable informa-tion, so that a paper only system is not really recommended—although *anything* is better than nothing!

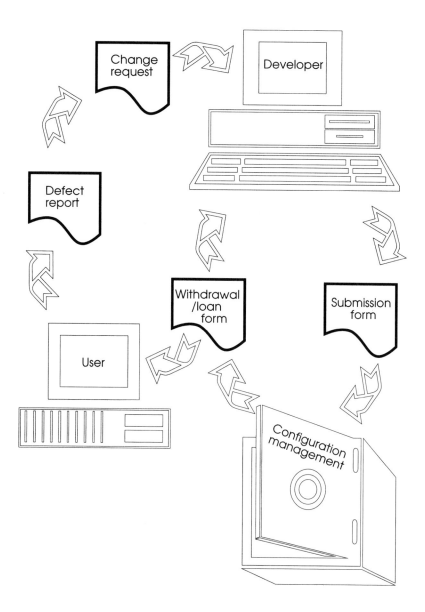

Figure 5.2   The CI life cycle controlled by forms

SUMMARY

No one would dream of refusing to supply an engineer with sufficient disc space to develop code, of not allowing a technical author access to a suitable word processor, or of not supplying a secretary with a filing cabinet, but trying to get the *right facilities* for CM to operate as efficiently as possible is sometimes like getting the proverbial 'blood out of a stone'.

> One candidate configuration controller described the system he was running to an interviewer, who was fascinated to hear about the illogical mixture of manual and automated methods the candidate was having to work with; all the configuration control forms were electronic, with unique numbers allocated automatically by the tool they were using. This sounded fine but then they had to log all the forms manually because the server they were using was 'down' more often than not and, even when it was running, was so slow that it was actually quicker to thumb through paper files than to interrogate the forms database!

Obviously, a CM system can only be implemented properly if the staff have the right experience, are adequately trained and are sufficient in number. Before this can be achieved, the job specifications have to be clearly defined—not only for individuals applying for specific CM jobs but for the entire IT industry. Clear career paths have to be mapped out that will attract the right sort of applicants and then keep them! The office accommodation for the CM team and the computer facilities *must* be both sufficient and central for immediate but controlled access by all the project, through the electronic, document and reference libraries.

CM procedures must be set in place that are appropriate to the complexity of the individual project, with configuration control forms supplying the medium for data collection and reporting to enable the library functions to run smoothly. The next chapter, which covers the various interfaces to CM from other project sections, shows how important all this is.

6

PROJECT INTERFACES

- SENIOR MANAGEMENT
- THE CUSTOMER
- SUB-CONTRACTORS
- FINANCE AND PROGRAMME CONTROL
- CONTROL BODIES
- TECHNICAL AUTHORITY
- SYSTEM SUPPORT/ENVIRONMENT BUREAU
- THE DEVELOPMENT TEAMS
- TECHNICAL DOCUMENTATION TEAMS
- TEST AND ACCEPTANCE
- QUALITY ASSURANCE
- SUMMARY

Many excellent configuration control systems exist where engineers run version, build and access control systems for the software, or where hardware inventories are controlled against 'goods in' and subsequent maintenance. But these are not usually expanded to be part of overall project CM, which incorporates software, hardware and the documentation, includes the contract(s) or SLA(s) and requirements, and sub-contractor/customer deliverables. In Chapter 4, we saw how CM is the single continuous function which links all phases of a project, and in this chapter we look at the interfaces between CM and all sections of project personnel (from junior engineers to project managers and the customer).

In order to illustrate these interfaces, typical job titles have been used which may or may not exist in your organization. Just because your project does not have anyone called, for example, 'Technical Authority' does not mean to say that the role does not exist— even if the tasks and the responsibilities are actually handled by someone with a different title or even several people rather than one. So, in reading this chapter, concentrate on the role rather than the job title.

SENIOR MANAGEMENT

Unfortunately, often the first time senior management become aware of CM on a project is when they are asked to approve a budget for a CM tool or personnel.

Unless the project manager has been fortunate enough to experience a good CM system on previous projects, this part of the overall budget may be rejected outright or, if the customer or a standard such as ISO 9001 dictates, only grudgingly approved. The project manager on a large project may never become aware of how the CM system is helping the design and development engineers and, in fact, may be under the misconception that, were it not for CM, the delivery timescales could be shorter! It is not surprising then that project management may have a mere tolerance of, rather than backing for, CM since often only the complaints filter up to them, not the successes. Another problem is that, because senior management are sometimes unaware of exactly how a CM system should work or even may be working on their own project, they are the first to break the rules and can force a configuration manager to abandon procedures, by 'pulling rank'!

> One configuration manager needed to make a minor modification to the timescales of part of a contract, on a very large project he was working on, and so started progressing the requisite change request. The procedures dictated that every customer-impact change had to be fully documented and reviewed internally, by the technical sections of the project, before the proposed change could be escalated to the commercial and senior management and, certainly, long before it was passed to the customer.
>
> This particular change had been left rather late and, despite warnings, the project manager said, 'Never mind the procedures, I don't believe it impacts anything but the commercial annexes of the contract, so we'll skip the technical review—there's just not enough time'. The costed change went to the customer, but the configuration manager insisted that they do the technical review in background mode anyway. Inevitably, they found that the supposedly purely financial and timescale changes would, in fact, have a serious impact on their technical ability to deliver another part of the system. So they had to withdraw the change request, re-review both the technical and commercial aspects of the proposed change and re-submit. All of which not only took considerably longer than it would, had they followed the procedures properly in the first place, but it also made them look foolish in front of the customer. The same project manager insisted on bypassing the procedures several more times over the following two years and, without exception, each time was a disaster! At last she came to

understand why the procedures were needed and how they were designed *not* to hinder, but to *save time and money*.

One of the most spectacular muck-ups that helped educate another project manager, started with the almost inevitable instruction to skip the procedures.... Again, despite strong objections from the configuration manager, the project manager allowed part of the contract to be updated and signed off at the customer site in what was called an 'Addendum', without having progressed the requisite change request or having involved the configuration control board (CCB) in reviewing the update. A few weeks later the project failed a delivery inspection test because the customer wanted to know where the 'support equipment' was. 'What support equipment?', asked the acceptance team, surprised, as they knew the contract inside out and knew there was no mention of this in it, as can be seen from the following extract:

Clause 33 Training and Support Acceptance
　　　　Training Equipment
　　　　– Office Automation　December 1989
　　　　– Communications　　March 1990

Unfortunately, when changing the delivery dates in the 'Addendum', the secretary typing up the changes had skipped a line and, as a result of the non-procedural update described above, the contract now read:

Clause 33 Training and Support Equipment
　　　　– Office Automation　December 1989
　　　　– Communications　　June 1990

The customer argued long and hard against accepting that the change (which could not have occurred had the update been the result of a properly reviewed and approved change request) had been made in error. They not only delayed the acceptance and therefore *payment* milestone by months, but also, at one stage, looked like insisting on delivery of the bogus 'support equipment' which would have cost the Project a lot of money! This was a hard way for that project manager to learn his lesson but, following this incident, he was far more supportive of the CM function!

This example also, of course, had a strong impact on the contracts manager, who had even less tolerance of CM than the project manager and used to announce, proudly, 'Of course I've got nothing against the configuration manager personally, but I can't stand CM or see the point of it'. Unlike the project manager, though, this contracts manager never did understand, despite devastating evidence! Fortunately, not all contracts managers are that blind or stubborn and there are many companies in which the contracts personnel regularly give excellent legal advice on the implications of change and use CM to the full, to control their contractual or SLA documents (including such items as consultancy rates and dates), so that they and the respective customers and sub-contractors know exactly what the contractual baselines are at any given point in the projects. (There is more about contract change control in Chapter 10.)

Another interface between senior management and CM may be on the issue of security. Obviously, in defence systems, the CIs may be classified as 'restricted' or above but, even on purely commercial contracts, there may be a necessity to ensure commercial confidentiality through careful access control and CI labelling. Comprehensive CM can be particularly useful on highly classified projects and, in fact, one of the best CM standards is the 'CESG Computer Security Memorandum No. 7' (CESG, 1990), which addresses 'Configuration Management for Secure Systems'. Classifications vary widely between organizations and governments but, typically, classifications would include 'unclassified', 'restricted', 'confidential' and 'secret', where each imposes increasing restrictions on the number and type of people/roles who have access to the classified item.

If you have worked on any secure systems, you will know that the security classification of the most highly classified item imposes a 'system high' on the total configuration. This means, for example, that if all the documentation and code files held on a processor or network are classified as 'restricted', except for one document which is 'confidential', then *all* the documentation and code on that processor or network have to be subjected to 'confidential' level controls. This, of course, can result in an enormous escalation (and therefore cost increase) of security procedures and facilities. CM can help such a situation because it can identify not only every item, but also the individual CIs' classifications and, from that information, the total system CI classification. It is then relatively simple to extract the few highly classified items and load them onto a stand-alone processor or perhaps tape or disc, leaving the 'system high' as only 'restricted'.

A similar situation can arise with change control, where it may be necessary to segregate a change request physically from a highly classified document which is to be changed. Good CM systems lend themselves easily to up- or down-grade of security classification, simply because everything (whether code or document files in a directory, hard copy documents, hardware inventories, drawings, or even tapes and discs) will be uniquely identified and traceable and, of course, subject to access control. This is one of the reasons why the defence and space industries have such a head start, in terms of CM, over systems which are not safety- or security-critical.

The truest test of CM's value to senior management is one that, hopefully, will never be proven; that of recovery from total disaster.

> A few years ago a large office block in Hampshire went up in flames and literally everything—computers, documents, discs and tapes, furniture but, thankfully, no people—was totally destroyed in less than a couple of hours. A configuration controller visited the site only days after the disaster and now, as a configuration manager, makes a point of keeping it in mind when doing a mental audit of any CM system, to ensure that everything it controls—whether the CIs themselves and all their versions, inventories on them, forms affecting them, proof of signatures and dates approving them, or minutes of meetings about them—is held electronically and, through system support back-ups, is safeguarded in fire safes and off-site.

With this comprehensive and protected database, recovery from an event such as fire should literally be a question of obtaining the latest back-up from the fire safe (or, if even that has been destroyed, then the off-site storage), reloading and printing out reports and forms from the electronic copies, to establish the system configuration status and to prove that soft copies of all the CIs—in actual or inventory format— have been correctly restored in the controlled area.

The ITIL CM Module (CCTA, 1990) advocates setting up an awareness campaign in a project, when introducing CM:

> Make it clear in the awareness campaign that there is senior manage- ment commitment to configuration management—invite senior management to give the opening address at seminars, to sign leaflets and in general to 'lead from the front'.

This would be ideal but, unfortunately, there is a 'Catch-22' situation at the moment, whereby some senior managers still need convincing themselves!

THE CUSTOMER

One of the best ways of convincing senior management is to convince the customer or user. Because a good CM system is so proceduralized and by its very nature so reliable, it is easy to demonstrate, to show the customer how efficient the defect reporting and change control systems are, and how customer requests for changes to the requirement are flowed up to contract changes and down to design and code changes. This can give them great confidence in the supplier's ability to deliver. At acceptance tests, for example, a customer is almost more impressed with a small list of declared 'known deficiencies', clearly documented with how and when they will be cleared and what they impact, than by simply being assured that the whole deliverable works to perfection.

Customers, once educated in the reasons for CM procedures, should be the strongest supporters, since they can then satisfy themselves, for example, that sufficient impact analysis is being carried out which will reduce the number of errors found, minimize the redevelopment time and ensure a more easily maintainable delivered system. If more customers over the past 20 years had insisted on CM in their contracts and had accepted that sufficient cost had to be built into the price to cover proper CM, this book would not be necessary.

SUB-CONTRACTORS

A configuration manager must establish a clear interface with sub-contractors too, of course. This is to ensure that CIs delivered from them are of the required quality, that timescales for deliveries can be monitored and met, and that problems or possible defects can be identified and corrected as early as possible. It is a good idea to issue a formal 'sub-contractor CM requirements' document, setting out:

- exactly what degree of CM is required for a particular sub-contractor,
- what disciplines/standards they will be expected to follow, and
- a clause ensuring that the sub-contractor will issue a list of CIs for delivery, in their answering CM plan.

The sub-contractor's CM plan can then be used to assess progress and the degree of compliancy, in CM audits. Again, the ITIL CM Module (CCTA, 1990) puts it succinctly, explaining what is required on receipt of sub-contractor deliverables (i.e. 'bought-in CIs'):

> Procedures must be planned for bought-in CIs, including hardware, communications equipment, documentation, software packages, operating systems software and utilities. Goods-inward procedures covering computer operations, network management, computer installation/acceptance, procurement and administrative staff must

ensure that all authorized new CIs are correctly registered in the CMDB before they are delivered and that the status of these CIs is changed as they are delivered, installed, tested, accepted, etc.

FINANCE AND PROGRAMME CONTROL

Another section of project personnel that can reap the benefits of CM is finance and programme control or planning. For example, CM should be able to supply a complete inventory of the hardware kit on any project and, in liaison with system support, be able to track the number of defects on delivered hardware and/or proprietary software, so that vendor reliability and maintenance standards can be analysed. If the right fields are built into change requests and defect reports, then programme control will be able to track estimated and actual time spent on a particular contractual, design or development change activity for cost statistics, and then use these metrics for planning future development or maintenance projects in terms of timescales and staff numbers (see Chapter 13).

There was absolute panic one afternoon on one project, when the planning manager received notification from the customer's auditors, that they were supposed to have delivered copies of the software that had been accepted at pre-delivery inspection, six months before—a contractual clause completely overlooked by them *and* the customer! This was not at the end of the project but halfway through, and so the whole development baseline had moved on considerably. By interrogating the CM database, it took literally only minutes for them to establish exactly what builds of software had been acceptance tested and to confirm the version of each and every file contained in those builds. It happened that some of the software had already been archived to tape, and as the tapes had been uniquely numbered and controlled by CM, these were easy to locate and copy. It was equally simple to withdraw the other software from the controlled area and copy it to tape as well, because the CI structure allowed for such a necessity (see Chapter 8). The tapes were ready for delivery within a couple of hours and, ironically, the most time-consuming activity of all had been the creation of the fancy sticky labels to put on the tapes!

What CM needs from the planning department in return for this sort of support is recognition of CM's value and, consequently, backing for sufficient time to be built in to the project timescales for all the CM activities to take place. CM should not be seen as the proverbial 'bottleneck', but as an essential and *planned* activity. There is a wonderful truism in Ashley and Team's *Starter Kit for Setting Up a Measurement Program* (1994), which should be printed in large letters on every project planner's office wall!

There's never time to do it right, but there's always time to correct it.

A large (300 man-year) project was starting to slip its internal milestones and so the software development group manager and team leaders held a briefing and brain-storming session to highlight the problems and to plan the way ahead. Figure 6.1 is one of the overhead projector (OHP) foils from that briefing and, although all the points made in it are typical of the sort of problems that face many projects, it is obviously the inclusion of configuration control that is of interest here.

Configuration control had been included because one of the component teams had claimed that the red tape of CM on the project

SOFTWARE DEVELOPMENT PROBLEMS

- With few exceptions, all software development continues to slip
- We are getting no nearer end dates
- Progress problems caused and worsened by:

  - Fragmentation
  - Efficiency
  - Reviews—editorial not technical
  - Ill-defined targets
  - Configuration control

ACTION NEEDED NOW FOR SUCCESSFUL DELIVERY OF QUALITY PRODUCT

Figure 6.1   OHP on software development problems

was one of the main reasons they had slipped badly. During the brain-storming session, however, the following facts emerged:

- none of the component teams' plans held a realistic contingency for rework/fault rectification;
- because time was tight, one of the teams had bypassed several steps in their dry run testing (see Chapter 9) not just on their first submission to CM, but on the submission of the supposedly corrected software, and this had resulted in a large number of defect reports and change requests having to be raised, reviewed and cleared, which should have been avoided; and
- some of the teams had not followed the project procedures (for reviews, CM, planning, etc.) properly, which caused duplication of work, and it was found that the team members were actually guessing what needed to be done, because the team leader had the procedures locked away in a cupboard!

The conclusion drawn by the group manager was that none of the slippage could be said to be due to CM, but to poor planning and to the incorrect (or total lack of) use of project procedures.

CONTROL BODIES

One of the most obvious opportunities for interface between the customer or subcontractors, senior management, the commercial and planning departments and CM is offered by the configuration control board (CCB). This is the formal forum for discussion, review and approval of change requests affecting the high-level CIs such as the contract and sub-contracts, SLAs, procurement or requirements documents and other deliverables. Items such as cost, timescales and baselines should also be discussed, in terms of establishing exactly what will constitute a particular delivery and how acceptability will be proven. In other words, what is being delivered, when, and what test procedures are going to be followed.

It is important that CM prepare this body of senior, and therefore expensive, personnel for each CCB by ensuring that all relevant information (such as copies and/or registers of change requests, lists of planned updates to the high-level CIs, etc.) is passed to them in plenty of time for review prior to the meeting, so that only the most contentious issues need be discussed. This preparation is important because much time can be wasted otherwise, but it has to be *proactive*.

> The only reason one project had CCB meetings was because chocolate biscuits used to be served! The group managers there used to spend hours arguing whether or not they had seen a particular change request that was due for sign off and often, because they had no sense of 'Team', used to waste much valuable time by blaming each other's groups for delays, instead of working together to avoid them.

If the customer is external (e.g. another company or a foreign government, as opposed to another department) it will be necessary to have two levels of control board (see Figure 6.2): one, as described above but named the customer configuration review board (CCRB) and one, the CCB, at which the contractor/supplier 'gets his act together', in terms of costs and prices, timescales, etc., before passing on quotations. Formal minutes must be taken of these CCRBs and signed by the chairmen, since decisions made and recorded at the meetings may end up being used, for *legal* purposes, to prove exactly where, when and by whom important decisions were made, if the project starts slipping or the customer gets difficult! (Suggested agendas for these and other control board meetings are given in Appendix A.12.)

Underneath the (CCRB and) CCB which, as stated above, are concerned with customer-related issues, there needs to be a body of technical expertise whose role is to review and approve defect reports, baselines, CIs and their structures and change requests from the technical, rather than contractual, angle. This technical review committee (TRC) might only meet once a month in the early stages of a large project and then, once development starts, once per week for just one hour. The meetings must be regular, but short and sharp, and it is essential that the committee members always prepare for them in advance by checking registers and reviewing forms. The agenda for these TRC meetings should cover items such as review of those defect reports and change requests raised since the last meeting (see Appendix A.12). This ensures that all forms are completed as accurately and fully as possible early on and are planned for clearance in an appropriate future baseline (this is *not* an administrative exercise, by the way). The TRC should also check whether or not a particular problem has been raised elsewhere, in which case the defect report could be subsumed into an existing proposed CI update, thus saving many days of wasted effort in investigating it.

As with the CCRB and CCB, CM's role is to ensure that the TRC members have the right information to make the right decisions proactively and in time. This means ensuring that the database or manual logs of change requests and defect reports are always up-to-date and accurate and that registers are available (preferably on-line). The TRC members must be able to obtain information such as defect reports that

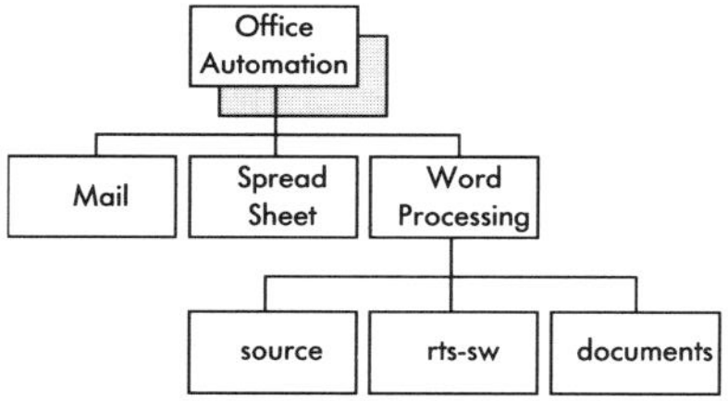

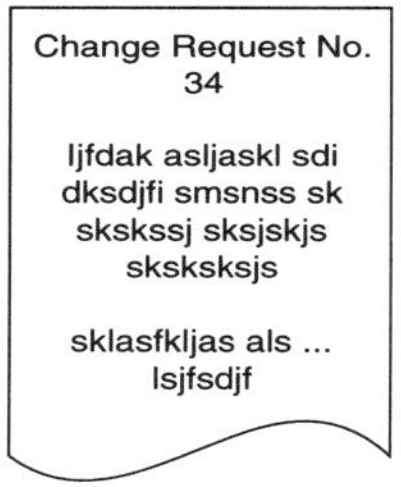

Board/Committee	Attendees	CIs Sign Off	Forms Sign Off
Customer Configuration Review Board (CCRB)	External Customers and Senior Project Management	Contracts, SLAs, Requirements Specifications	Customer Change Requests
Configuration Control Board (CCB)	Internal Customers and Senior Project Management	Contracts, SLAs, Requirements Specifications	Change Requests
Technical Review Committee (TRC)	Technical Support/ Development Team Leaders	Design Documents, Software, Drawings, Hardware	Change Requests, Defect Reports, Submission Forms

Change Request No. 34

lljfdak asljaskl sdi dksdjfi smsnss sk skskssj sksjskjs skskskjs

sklasfkljas als … lsjfsdjf

Office Automation

Mail

Spread Sheet

Word Processing

source

rts-sw

documents

Figure 6.2 The control boards

should have been actioned by a certain date but were overdue, what change requests impacted a particular build of software, etc. As the nature of the TRC should be far more informal than a CCRB or CCB, since it deals with all internal rather than customer-related CM issues, it is best not to attempt to sign-off the vast quantity of change requests and defect reports at the meetings themselves. The same body of people must be involved in the review and approval of the forms but, once forms have been identified at the TRC meetings and their baseline impact established, their further review and approval can take place 'ex-committee', so that the meetings are not bogged down with bureaucracy.

One of the CM team should act as secretary for CCRB, CCB and TRC meetings because such a person is best able to provide up-to-date information and, having project-wide interfaces, can progress information from one committee to the next, acting as point of contact for minuted actions. The chairman of the TRC could be the configuration manager, but a better candidate on a large project would be the 'technical authority'.

TECHNICAL AUTHORITY

This role may have another title in your organization (or may not even exist), but there is bound to be someone with the right experience who could fill the role, even if on a part-time basis. The job requisites are a sound technical and contractual knowledge of all the project requirements and deliverables, coupled with many years' project life cycle experience. The reason for having the technical authority or configuration manager as chairman of the TRC is that it is necessary to have an objective chair.

The gaggle of group managers, who used to spend their meetings eating chocolate biscuits and blaming each other, was not a good example of how a project team should work but neither was it exceptional, unfortunately. Even the best project members will try to avoid taking on extra work for their teams when timescales are critically tight, and they may not be able to be sufficiently objective in matters such as baseline planning. For example, one component team may not have time to include a new function in a particular build, whereas another team may need to interface to it in order to complete a scheduled activity. Only someone completely objective, like the technical authority, can evaluate the relative importance to the whole project of exactly when that new requirement should be included and, being objective, will not be swayed by individual component problems.

The same objectivity comes into play in defect reporting where, for example, an initial investigation may point to the reported fault lying with the software, but the software team declares that it is not their code, but the operating system or even hardware that is causing the fault. In this case, much time can be wasted by 'buck-passing' and it should rest with the technical authority, as TRC chairman, to evaluate the situation and decide which area or areas need to take corrective action.

SYSTEM SUPPORT/ENVIRONMENT BUREAU

The operating system is one of the most important CIs (since it impacts all the software being used, developed, maintained and tested and may impact the hardware too) but it gets forgotten most often. Configuration control of the environment (i.e. the operating system, compilers, packaged software, the hardware platforms, etc.) is a very important interface between CM and a project's system support group. And what a relief, when system support discover a virus, for them to be able to retrieve and restore a known, virus-free system configuration from the controlled area! Another, and perhaps the most essential interface, is the provision of back-ups for the total CM system, and yet another is support of whatever CM tool(s) is being used. Depending on the size and complexity of the project, maintenance of the CM tool in terms of software interfaces, customization and first-line help desk for users may rest with either the CM team or system support. It is essential that the CM team members have a thorough understanding of the CM tool(s) being used and can customize it themselves, but help will always be needed from system support for such events as processor crash recovery, disc partitioning, archiving, specific printing facilities, etc.

THE DEVELOPMENT TEAMS

And what of the development teams who, possibly, have the most to gain through well-run CM and the most to lose through a poor or non-existent CM system? As stated in Chapter 2, it used to be the engineers who fought longest and hardest against having their code and design documentation controlled but, over the past decade, there has been an ever-increasing support for CM from this area.

> An example of this was an upgrade to a CM tool, which included an ability to override the necessity to 'get for change'. In the 'two tier control system' that is advocated in the next chapter, this could have saved a lot of time, as the CIs in the formal area could be updated without having to set the 'change flag'. During evaluation of this upgrade, however, one of the development team leaders on a project stated categorically that unless this 'feature' could be disabled for all but the CM team, they should not upgrade. One might have expected him to welcome the time-saving for his team, but he was experienced and sensible enough to see the dangers that could have resulted in such weakening of control.

Developers now have the most to gain from access to the new generation of CM and software configuration control tools (see Chapter 14), which offer facilities such as build control, release management and file merging. The tools also give the whole team accurate and easy to use information on each other's CIs, together with the ability to script many of the more tedious, repetitive tasks associated with CM. It is essential not only to provide a good CM system for the development teams (and everyone else) interfacing to it, however, but also to give them sufficient *training* in use of the tools and the way the procedures work.

> One engineer was so concerned with following what he thought were the procedures that, during a period of three months or so, he raised something like fifty defect reports and change requests. Had he read the procedures more thoroughly, he would have found that the same number of faults could have been reported and cleared on a quarter of the number of forms, i.e. one change request could have cleared several defect reports. His relief when this was pointed out was almost comical, but the sad thing is that, because he had *expected* CM to be a pain, he had never questioned whether the time-consuming and somewhat illogical exercise he was going through was right!

It may, mistakenly, have been implied that it is always the CM team who are right and 'the rest' who get things wrong or would cheat if possible! The CM team do have to be extra careful and meticulous, as was said in the last chapter, but of course they make mistakes and sometimes these can cost a lot of time. In a good CM environment, however, every mistake is less costly and time-consuming than in a less controlled one, because it is so much easier to pinpoint exactly what has gone wrong and where and, also, plan exactly how much or how little re-submission, rebuilding or retesting is necessary to obviate the error. Also, of course, once the mistake has been traced it is often possible to build some small step into a procedure that will mean that it will not happen again (*vive le process improvement!*).

TECHNICAL DOCUMENTATION TEAMS

Depending on the size or set-up of a particular company or project, production of technical/user documentation may be through a technical documentation department, a team of technical authors, the development team themselves or, perhaps, the development team plus secretaries. Whoever is responsible, the documents are CIs, and their authors sometimes do not realize that they, too, must comply with the configuration control procedures.

For example, one company took on a highly qualified technical author who had never worked in a fixed-price project before, but only in a technical documentation department of a large company. She was justifiably proud of the standard of her own work but could not see that, now she was part of a project, she was bound by its procedures too. The CM procedures ensured that all CI documents were only updated by implementing fully approved change requests, but trying to get this lady to restrict her updates to 'the *approved changes, all* the approved changes and *nothing but* the approved changes,' was almost impossible, because she would constantly improve the grammar, correct layout inconsistencies, etc., thus compromising the exact traceability from change request to update, and really unnerving their customer.

Document production nowadays has ever-increasing automated functionality (e.g. building in FrameMaker (TM), data modelling in Software through Pictures (TM), the encapsulation of diagrams from packages such as Visio (TM) into word processors such as Wordperfect (TM)). This means that the configuration control facilities described in this book are becoming just as applicable and essential to technical authors as to 'code cutters', since lack of version control, access control, traceability, etc., can be just as much a problem for the implementation of document changes as they are for software.

TEST AND ACCEPTANCE

Obviously there is going to be a close interface between CM and test and acceptance (T&A), because no CI should ever be formally tested that has not come direct from the controlled area, and the test programs and data and even the test environment should all be under control. Prior to testing particular CIs, T&A should be able to interrogate control forms for information on what defects are still outstanding, and when these defects are planned for clearance. At the start of testing, CM should supply T&A with full build state logs of the CIs under test, listing their structures, file versions, change status and overall build/baseline numbers. Then, during testing, there is another vital interface because, with sound configuration control, part re-testing is possible if defects are found (see Chapter 11).

The phrase 'what defects are still outstanding' may need explanation, as it is yet another misconception that items should only be put under control once they are 'correct'. While this is true of the majority of CIs, and is certainly desirable, allowance must be made for submitting items that are known to be less then perfect. For example, only three out of the four module chapters in a component human–computer interface (HCI) specification may have been written, but software modules 1 to 3 are ready for formal test. In this case, the HCI document should be issued, with a defect report opened against it reflecting that Chapter 4 is still to be added. The formal test of modules 1 to 3 can then take place, using the document at Issue 1.00 (with known deficiencies that obviously do not impact this test) and the document would only have to be updated, clearing the defect report, before software module 4 is tested. Similar situations could arise with the submission of code, with certain elements being submitted as 'stubs', or with an incomplete hardware configuration.

QUALITY ASSURANCE

The interface to QA has been left until last, to accentuate its overall 'guardianship' of any project or, indeed, organization. You may have been wondering what QA was doing to allow the procedure-skipping described in the opening paragraphs of this chapter. Well, sadly, the answer in those particular project cases was absolutely nothing! Many quality managers—and these were no exception—report directly or indirectly to the project managers and are, thus, just as subject to 'rank pulling' as any other project member. What *should* happen is that the QA function in an organization is divorced from any particular project and reports directly to the managing director or department head, so that they have no vested interest in lowering standards. When this is the case, the configuration manager, test and acceptance manager, or whoever is being pressurized to skip the procedures, can resort to asking QA to investigate and prevent such occurrences.

As mentioned in Chapter 3, CM is not a part of quality assurance in terms of line management. The configuration manager is, of course, responsible for building quality *control* into all CM processes, just like any other project activity. No configuration manager can operate successfully without a sound knowledge and understanding of the QA function, either, and it can, obviously, be extremely helpful when writing a CM plan or set of procedures, if the quality manager is both able and willing to advise on policy and standards.

What benefits are there to QA, in a sound CM system? For a start, all the requisite data for defect analysis should be readily available (preferably in electronic format which can be searched and sorted on different criteria) and, of course, CM should offer clear traceability of every version of every CI and of all configuration control forms affecting them. When QA are called upon to ratify decisions taken by the CCB or TRC, to witness the transfer of CIs for acceptance testing from the controlled area, or to confirm that a CI is of a sufficiently high quality to warrant delivery, a conscientious quality manager will have a far happier time and feel far more confident about putting the seal of approval on items that have been well controlled, than if CM has been absent or of a questionable standard.

SUMMARY

Looking back at this chapter, it would appear that the only people who do not interface in any way to CM are the cleaners! Senior management are concerned with how much it will cost and how much it will save; they are concerned with control of changes to the contracts or SLAs and any impacts on security; and, although the chances of total disaster are small, senior management should be insisting that CM provide one of the mechanisms for total recovery.

The customers (whether external such as another company or a government, or internal such as another department or directorate) should be insistent on having a comprehensive CM system so that they can track how the project is progressing, can see the full impact of proposed changes to the contract and, finally, can be assured of minimal maintenance problems regardless of whether they or the contractor/supplier are going to be responsible for it.

For much the same reasons, suppliers should insist that their sub-contractors have good CM systems which, in turn, will help finance, planning and programme control and all these bodies should be brought together through customer and/or configuration control boards (CCRBs and CCBs). Another type of control board, which is internal only, is the technical review committee (TRC) and this brings together the development teams and test and acceptance, guided by an objective technical authority, so that the project can keep abreast of all the defects being reported and the changes being requested and can plan which baselines they will be cleared in and, therefore, tested in.

Support functions like system support or the environment bureau and the technical documentation team also play a part in ensuring that CM runs smoothly and, finally, quality assurance can only have real confidence in the items it 'stamps' if they have been controlled meticulously through CM. Exactly what those items should be—in other words, what is and is not a CI—is handled in the next chapter.

7

WHAT DOES AND DOES NOT NEED CONTROLLING?

- DEFINITION OF A CI
- ONE ITEM OR A COLLECTION
- EXAMPLE CIs
- WHAT IS *NOT* A CI?
- TWO-TIER CONTROL
- THE CI PLAN
- SUMMARY

DEFINITION OF A CI

Look carefully at the following definition of what a configuration item (CI) is, in theory, and then we will work out what one would be, in practice:

A configuration item (CI) is any part of the development and/or deliverable system (whether software, hardware, firmware, drawings, inventories and/or documentation) which needs to be independently identified, stored, tested, reviewed, used, changed, delivered and/or maintained. CIs differ widely in complexity and may contain other CIs in a hierarchy.

The first important point made in the above is that it is not just the deliverables that are CIs. Test harnesses and data, for example, must be carefully controlled so that they can be used every time the CIs they test are modified, throughout the development phase and on into warranty and maintenance. It may not be usual to deliver design documentation but not to control it would be unthinkable. A prototype would probably not be delivered either, but it may form an essential part of the traceability of the system that was developed from it and so (particularly if the customer has had sight of it, or if the prototype is part of a rapid application development system) also needs to be carefully controlled.

ONE ITEM OR A COLLECTION

The next important word in the CI definition is 'independently', because a CI may be one item or a collection of items (i.e. a hierarchy). For example, a module CI might consist of hundreds of files; a component might be made up of many modules; there could be a large number of issued drawings itemized in a single drawings list CI; and the ultimate CI—the system itself—will consist of all the CIs of every type. Imagine a requirement specification for a large project, which has many volumes, each of which describes the various functional requirements of the project for both the application software and the target hardware. If there were a proposed change to the requirement, the first question that would be asked is 'does the change affect the hardware or the software?' and the change request would probably be routed to entirely different people for review, depending on the answer. The sensible items to identify as CIs in this case, therefore, would be the requirement specification *volumes* (so that change requests could be investigated in parallel and each volume updated *independently* of the others). There might, of course, be proposed changes which impact more than one volume of the requirement specification, but this would be handled by cross-referencing or linking the CIs, which is dealt with in Chapters 8 and 10.

The point is that there is no hard and fast rule about what a CI comprises, because while it would be correct to divide this requirement specification into lower-level CIs, it would be total overkill to treat each of the sections of a low-level design document as individual CIs. What is important is to ensure that every level of granularity offers *added value*, because it will certainly add extra effort to control. Chapter 8 goes into detail on how and why CIs should be structured, and this is based entirely on the value of any one CI's independence from other CIs. Another example of differing granularity is a sub-contractor's deliverable hardware. Hopefully the sub-contractor has all the kit's design, development and deliverable items under configuration control and that will mean hundreds of CIs in the sub-contractor's CM system. From the prime contractor's point of view, however, there may only be a few CIs, because the contractor is only interested at 'black box' level.

A senior sales executive from a large company set off by air to Dublin (no, this is *not* an Irish joke) with a tape in his briefcase, to give a demonstration to a banking organization that was on the verge of signing a significant contract. About ten minutes after he had taken off, someone realized that although he had the correct prototype to demonstrate, he had taken the version for the Sunos (TM) operating system whereas the banking organization used Hewlett-Packards. The requisite tape had actually been created but, because the variants had not been logged in any form of configuration control system, it had been too easy to 'grab' the wrong tape, which resulted in the executive having to turn round at Dublin airport and go back to fetch the correct version.

This was costly in terms of airfare and senior management time and also, far more importantly, did not do a lot for the company's image with the potential customer. It is an interesting point here, that not only should the prototype have been a CI, but the *medium* on which it was stored should also have been uniquely identified within a CM system, so that it was obvious that 'Tape No. NNN' contained 'Prototype (version nnn) for the XXX System' for use on the 'SSS Operating System (version mmm)'—all of which should, preferably, have been held in a database for the sales executive to interrogate and then check against the tape that had been handed to him. The data entries required for configuration management of transfer media (i.e. tapes and discs) are few and simple, but no less essential and are documented in Appendix A.14.

Back to the CI definition: many projects make the mistake of carefully controlling their source code and its documentation, forgetting completely that a component tested on one version of an operating system may fall over if run on an upgrade. Likewise, components built with one version of a compiler may fail if the compiler is modified. For example, three different versions of a compiler were found to be being used on one project before it became subject to CM, and just putting that compiler under configuration control, so that all the teams used the same version, resolved a large number of defect reports! It is no use carefully controlling the source code, either, if its resulting run-time system—on whatever media—is not controlled and its use proceduralized (as happened with a target engagement system component which kept falling over during testing because, although all the CIs were under control, the engineers were not—they had not checked the label numbers on the PROM chips before installing them and were using the wrong versions!).

The environment bureau (or system support, as it is known in some companies) were quite the worst for ignoring CM on one project and kept trying to avoid submitting their environment CIs (i.e. operating systems, compilers, proprietary software packages, hardware platform inventories, configuration files, etc.) to CM or following any CM procedures, if at all possible. One of the worst culprits left the project and, in his farewell speech, actually joked about the rigours of CM being one of the reasons for his going. He was a sociable chap and kept in touch with many of the engineers and, after about four months in his new company, he sent the following message to the configuration manager. 'Although it hurts badly to admit it, you were right. They've never even heard of configuration control here and I now understand what the hell you were on about!'

EXAMPLE CIs

Below are some examples of CIs, as listed in a recent CM plan:

- contracts, SLAs and sub-contracts;
- technical documents, including all deliverables to the customer and/or sub-contractors (e.g. the procurement specification, acceptance test plan) and including component test plans, specifications, procedures and reports;
- standards and procedures which affect the technical aspects of the project (e.g. 'C' coding standards, change control procedures, QA plan) but not those of a purely administrative nature (e.g. procedure for the production of minutes, health and safety standards);
- deliverable software and all directly associated development software (including test data, harnesses, stubs, diagnostics, test programs, development tools and templates);
- inventories of proprietary software used in the development and test environments and on-site (e.g. word processors, operating systems, tools, compiler(s));
- standards for and inventories of hardware for the development and test environments and for delivery;
- sub-contractor supplied hardware inventories, drawings, documentation and software, which may be in soft and/or hard copy format, which affects the technical aspects of the project (e.g. sub-contractor CM plans, component software), but excluding non-bespoke proprietary manuals, user guides, etc.;
- baselined drawings;
- demonstrations to the customer, which are linked to contract agreement and/or system acceptance (e.g. presentation foils, brochures and prototypes).

That is a long list of what should be controlled, and if the list of categories is allowed to grow much longer, then the effort required to control it may become untenable. It is very important to remember that over-zealousness can be nearly as crippling as lack of control and this applies both to the timing and degrees of control (as discussed in Chapter 4), as well as to the items themselves.

WHAT IS *NOT* A CI?

What about what should *not* be under CM, then? You may have noticed that there was a caveat 'of a purely administrative nature' in the above list of CIs. This is a clue as to what can be left to the far less rigorous controls of team or central filing system review, distribution and back-ups. A good guideline for establishing whether or not something should be a CI is to ask 'Would our ability to deliver the right system, on time and within budget, be impacted in any way if a particular document, drawing, piece of software or hardware kit were lost or corrupted, or were used incorrectly or at the wrong version?'

On the whole, letters, memos, minutes, project notices, and administrative standards and procedures would *not* impact system delivery, although care must of course be taken to ensure they are easily retrievable when needed. It is not necessary to make them part of the CM system, because such disciplines as defect reporting and change control would be inappropriate for these items, which have nothing to do with the system configuration. There is, as always, a grey area in that letters or minutes *about* CIs or configuration control forms should not be treated as CIs themselves and yet, obviously, need to be linked to the CM system. In this case, a sensible cross-reference in terms of keyword or identifier should be more than sufficient. It is a good idea to maintain a filing category which is not strictly part of the CM system but related to it, called 'NNNNN Correspondence', where 'NNNNN' is a configuration control form type so that, for example, all correspondence and quotations relating to 'Contract Change Request No. 12' can be immediately located and reviewed with the change request itself.

Actually, a lot depends on the efficiency of the respective team and/or project, in deciding if it is essential that some items become CIs.

> The quality manager mentioned in Chapter 2 refused to put his quality plans for the various projects under CM (saying it was *his* responsibility as quality manager to control the quality plans, not CM's). As the project managers were his subordinates, they could not argue but, after Issues 1.00, 2.00 *and* 3.00 of a particular project's quality plan had all gone 'Absent without official leave (AWOL)' and had to be typed in again from hard copy, each time the plan was updated, the project manager involved created enough fuss to ensure that, from then on, the plan was put under CM!

DIFFERENT CONTROLS

Having defined the items that are 'CIs' and 'non-CIs', it is important to ensure that totally different controls are imposed which, in turn, necessitate staff with totally different experience and qualifications.

> One project director simply would not appreciate this difference and insisted that every document (whether CI or non-CI) should be

controlled by the project's central filing system. The filing clerks did a great job with letters, minutes, faxes and telephone messages but, as none of them was trained in CM in any way, the CI documents were filed with no thought of version or access control. They had no concept of master and copy, no knowledge of the documents' relationships to each other and the system configuration and, above all, no verification that what was being submitted to them for 'control' had been reviewed, was complete and/or had any known deficiencies.

The CM team had all the soft copies of the CI documents under their control, but had to control the hard copies by literally setting up a *rival* document library, using photocopies of the documents instead of the masters. This resulted in enormous frustration and duplication of effort, not only on the part of those controlling the two systems, but also on the poor beggars interfacing to them as they had to duplicate their document submissions—the hard copy master and 'Copy 1' to the central filing system and a second hard copy to CM. Had it not been for their support in the latter, serious problems would have arisen because, for example, when a document was lost by the central filing system or the wrong version of one distributed, the CM team were always able to produce a copy of the correct version. This is not, in any way, an indictment of the central filing staff, because they were not trained in CM and should never have been tasked with trying to emulate document configuration control. The indictment, in this case, rests solely with the project director who would not understand the difference between, and allow segregation of, the CIs from the non-CIs.

Think what actually happens to a CI (as illustrated in Figures 5.2 and 7.1) and the importance of segregating them from non-CIs will be more obvious. With both types of item, there is a develop/check/release-for-use cycle, but there is no reason to subject non-CIs to rigorous testing or review, defect reporting, version control, release management, impact analysis, status accounting, etc., while not to do so with CIs would, of course, be disastrous.

'STEPPING STONE' ITEMS

Another example of what should not be held in the controlled area but which is not so obvious, is anything that can be categorized as a 'stepping stone'. For example, we have already established that source code and the run-time system software must be CIs, but there is no justification for the interim object files to take up space and time

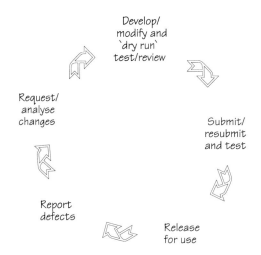

Figure 7.1   The life cycle of a CI

being controlled, as they serve no ongoing purpose. Scripts should therefore be written to clear down object files before source code is submitted.

One of the most interesting types of 'stepping-stone' which should not be classified as CIs is the data created by CASE tools, for such purposes as requirements traceability or software design. There are many CASE tools on the market and most have their own in-built control mechanisms to safeguard against accidental loss or parallel update and it needs to be clearly understood that the *data* created, used and stored by these tools is *not* subject to configuration control. What *is* subject is the *resulting item*, such as a requirements specification, design document, etc. So, it is best not to attempt to dump quantities of data into the already overburdened CM database, but to leave control of this to the respective CASE tool. Anyway, it would actually be dangerous to try to control the data outside the CASE tool, since submitting it to the CM library, and then extracting it for update by copying it back to the CASE tool, would probably fail miserably, as the CASE tool's database is likely to have become incompatible with that particular set of data in the meantime!

TWO-TIER CONTROL

Most projects suffer from the 'too much too soon' or 'too little too late' syndromes, because CM is usually introduced either *too early* in the project life cycle (thus imposing unnecessary constraints on the development teams before their items are anywhere ready for formal test or release), or *too late* (thus losing critical traceability because they have ignored CM altogether during development and tried to slip in a token sense of control just before delivery). To avoid this problem, configurations should be controlled on two levels, i.e. *formal* configuration control (total CM) and *development* configuration control (version control only). Both should be applied from project start-up to its final archive at the end of the contractual life cycle, but the controls will differ and two separate—but structurally identical—controlled areas should be set up, as illustrated in Figure 7.2.

The earlier chapters have all concentrated on formal CM and the top 'polo' in Figure 7.2 shows the CIs at formal issue, i.e. they are under the control of the CM team and can be released for use by other development teams, for formal test or for delivery to the customer. The middle 'polo' introduces a duplicate controlled area, however, where development engineers can use all the advantages of the respective CM system's and tool's version and access controls, reporting facilities, and repeatability and traceability functions, but *without being hampered* by any 'red tape'. For example, permission to change an item in the development controlled area may depend solely on the developer of that piece of software or document, and no change request would need to be raised or approved for implementation of the change, which can be tried and tested, and changed again and again, until the 'owner' is satisfied that it is correct. Only when the developer wants to progress the change of the item to the *formal* controlled area, must there be compliance with the CM procedures through the use of the configuration control forms (as illustrated in Figure 5.2).

Setting up this 'two-tier control' will depend on the platforms involved and the tools used. The duplicated areas might be on separate servers with copies of the tool installed on each (and with the link to formal CM being via tapes/discs), or on one server or LAN/WAN environment. The segregation between formal and development areas may be imposed by a procedural or an automated life cycle (i.e. workflow) and applicable access controls.

When exactly should a CI progress from development to formal configuration control? It is usually when it is at issue as opposed to draft status, but it could also be when it has reached any/all of the following stages:

(a) it is a document or inventory CI which has been formally reviewed (e.g. it is at Issue 1.00);
(b) it is a hardware or software CI that has been successfully dry-run tested and is ready for formal testing;
(c) it needs to be 'used' by a person/group other than its 'owner' (e.g. another team needs to interface to it) with declared 'known deficiencies'; and/or
(d) it is a document, a drawing or inventory CI which needs to be delivered to the customer and/or sub-contractor(s) for review, prior to reaching formal issue status.

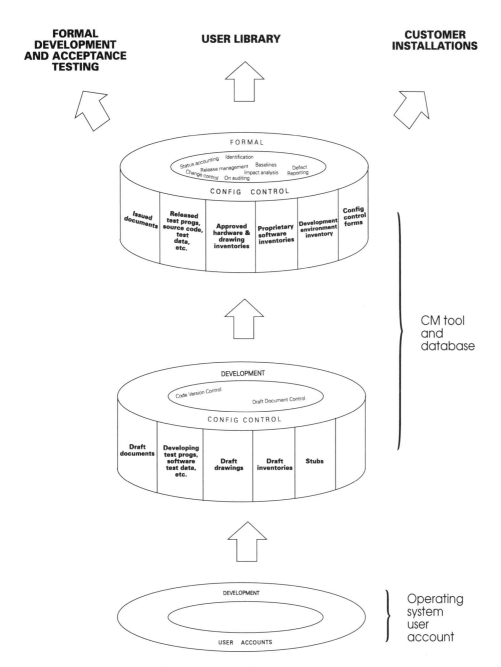

Figure 7.2   Two-tier configuration control

To illustrate use of the three 'polos', imagine an 'office automation' component containing a module on 'Registration', which has been fully designed and now needs implementing. The engineer will start writing the code in his/her own user area on the operating system and, obviously, will have several attempts at it—e.g. Versions

1 to 3—before having any confidence that the code matches the design (see Figure 7.3). At this point, the code should be submitted to the engineer's development controlled area with a version number like '1.00A' or 'First Draft'. The developer will then continue over a period of time, testing and correcting the module and perhaps, for every half-dozen 'saves' in the operating system user account, will submit another draft to the development controlled area.

During this phase, long before the code for the Registration module is ready for formal test, another team (that has been using a stub as an interface until then) may want to use the latest draft for an informal test of their own component. Because the module is under development control, not formal, the interfacing team will be fully aware that it comes to them 'warts and all' but, because the draft module is being controlled in the CM database by the CM tool, they will be able to trace future changes to the module and choose to use further drafts or wait until the module is formally released (with or without known deficiencies).

At last, then, when the module has been successfully 'dry-run' tested (see Chapter 9) it can progress to the formal controlled area, from which it can be formally tested, used and/or delivered. This, of course, probably means that at some future stage it will need to be 'bug-fixed' or enhanced and the developer will then repeat the cycle of drafts and formal releases—as illustrated in Figure 7.3—and, in fact, may even have been experimenting with alternative designs in the meantime, a luxury not so easily available where a development controlled area does not exist.

The only disadvantage of this two-tier control is the use of disc space (as mentioned in Chapter 5), but the enormous advantage of getting the balance right between too little or too much control, throughout the project life cycle—by *maximizing* essential traceability and repeatability, while *minimizing* procedural constraint—far outweighs the cost of disc space. In fact, if space is tight, then early versions of CIs in the development area can be deleted or at least archived as they are unlikely to be required again, since all early versions at formal issue will be in the formal controlled area.

Another option is to consider the compression of CI files, as savings of up to 60 per cent can be obtained. If the compression and decompression are part of a submission/withdrawal script, it will not put an overhead on the engineer and will avoid introducing human error. Compression is not always the correct panacea for lack of disc space, however, as CIs can no longer be read on-line and the ease with which file versions can be compared or viewed is seriously compromised. Some CM tools also minimize space problems by either controlling only the 'deltas' (i.e. what has changed between versions) and/or by using symbolic links, so that many of the 'copies' are actually only virtual (see Chapter 14).

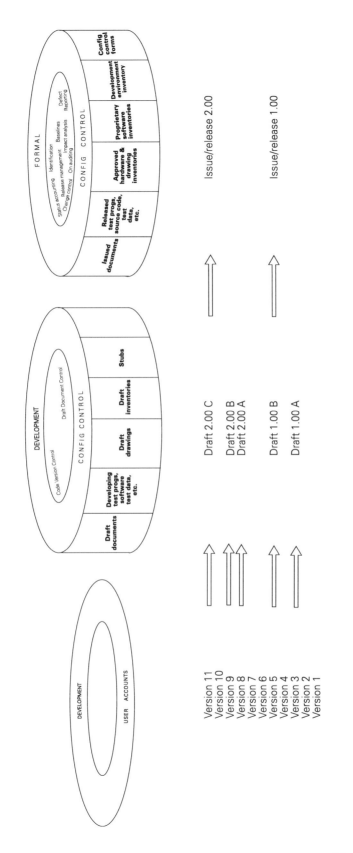

Figure 7.3   Version iterations, using two-tier control

THE CI PLAN

With the exception of correspondence and administrative documentation, then, most of the work done by project personnel will result in CIs. It is sound practice, therefore, to produce some sort of CI plan (which, like the snake swallowing its own tail, will also be a CI). The CI plan identifies early on in the project what CIs will be produced, at what level they will be controlled and which technical/commercial teams will be responsible for their production. With this high-level CI identification should be coupled the project-naming conventions for the CIs themselves (see Appendix A.4) and their planned production baselines (see Chapter 9).

SUMMARY

The definition of a configuration item at the beginning of this chapter was pretty extensive, but the main point made in the definition is that a CI is something that needs *individual* management or use. A CI is not necessarily a deliverable—as shown in the examples listed, such as test harnesses and development tools—but all deliverables are definitely CIs. What is also important to remember is to categorize what is *not* a CI and to impose different controls on the project's CIs and non-CIs because the requirements for access, traceability and reliability are entirely different and require entirely different personnel and procedures to manage them.

The concept of two-tier control for CIs was discussed so that the 'too much too soon' and 'too little too late' syndromes can be avoided, giving the developers all the power of a CM environment with none of the red tape, so that by the time the items (anticipated in the *CI* plan) are submitted to formal CM, they are of a far higher quality. To reiterate, then, the answer to 'what needs controlling?'—in other words, what is a CI?—is:

A configuration item (CI) is any part of the development and/or deliverable system (whether software, hardware, firmware, drawings, inventories and/or documentation) which needs to be independently identified, stored, tested, reviewed, used, changed, delivered and/or maintained. CIs differ widely in complexity and may contain other CIs in a hierarchy.

Even with a relatively small project, the CI plan is likely to identify several documents, software modules and components, lists of hardware kit and, possibly, installation drawings. Because it is the only way to cope with this quantity of items, it is absolutely essential to be able to categorize them and organize them into easily identifiable groups or hierarchies. The next Chapter shows how careful planning of the configuration structures can achieve just this.

8

PLAN THE STRUCTURES

- FLOWDOWN FROM THE CONTRACT
- CATEGORIZE THE CIs
- LINKING CIs
- MAINTENANCE STRUCTURES
- CONTROLLING THE STRUCTURES
- THE SYSTEM SPECIFICATION TREE (SST)
- SUMMARY

FLOWDOWN FROM THE CONTRACT

Not long after joining a company that specialized in Ministry of Defence (MoD) 'restricted' systems, their new configuration manager discovered what this really meant when he asked the four component team leaders of one of their major projects to draw him a simple diagram of what their components comprised. The results could have been hung in the Tate Gallery, entitled 'Meanderings of a Drunken Spider, Having Fallen in an Ink Pot' prompting the old joke 'Yes, but is it Art?'! The potential system was restricted all right—it was totally unintelligible even to those who were writing it. And when they did start to unravel it, they found gems like modules called for in the requirements specification which were not part of any of the components and calls to modules in other components that did not even exist. There was even one duplication, where two team leaders both thought they were responsible for one module's production!

So, relegate drunken spiders to the bathtub and make sure that you keep the flowdown from contract, to requirement, to component, to module very simple and easy to follow. A good test is 'if you can't draw it on the back of an envelope, it's too complicated', where 'it' could be the entire system, a component or a module in ever-increasing granularity. It is also recommended that no structure should ever be subdivided into more than seven levels because, for instance, if a module is that complicated it is probably best to hive off some of its functionality into a new module or modules. To see what is meant, look at Figure 8.1.

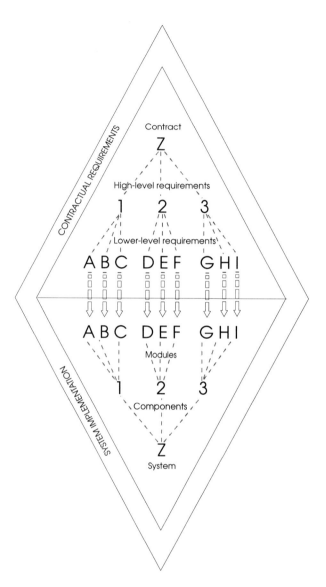

Figure 8.1   The requirements and implementation diamond

This diagram is simplicity itself, because it is so easy to map the overall contract to the resulting deliverable system, with each level being 'zoomed in on' to view what it, in turn, consists of. Then, once all the requirements are planned in the hierarchy, the corresponding modules can be planned, with the sub-components, components and finally the entire system implementation triangle, reflecting the contract's requirements. Next, if you invert this implementation triangle, you have the basic hierarchy of the system CI structure!

There are lots of ways of organizing the CI structures from here on, but the best is to take a sideways step and introduce *categories* of CIs, in other words to separate the controlled area into clear areas such as 'source', 'hardware', 'drawings', 'test', 'product', 'documentation', each of which is then subdivided into the respective project components from the implementation triangle of the diamond diagram.

It is traditional for software engineering teams to be left to their own devices to structure their components, and for them to divide the modules within those components into lower-level sub-directories such as 'src, bin and test' (see Figure 8.2). This keeps everything the individual engineer needs together in a convenient bundle and is, therefore, easy to develop as a stand-alone entity. But what happens when this entity becomes part of the greater whole—when it is integrated into a component and, then, into the complete system? What happens if the engineer from one component team moves on to another section of the project or, even worse, joins another company? How are those unfortunates, saddled with responsibility for maintenance, to find out not only what is causing a bug, but also where the relevant files are in a particular component's individualized structure, or how they relate to each other? And how can the boundaries of the system's source code be identified (either for a sizing exercise or for actual delivery) if it is fragmented into hundreds of little 'src' nodes under each individual module?

CATEGORIZE THE CIs

A panacea for these problems is to scrap the conventional, fragmented hierarchy and to standardize all of the high-level structures. This offers the component teams a template structure which they can then modify to suit their own particular component's idiosyncrasies, as part of the configuration identification exercise. This is done at the highest level, for software, by inverting the traditional 'src, bin, test' type directories, and bringing them from the bottom of the structure to the top, as illustrated in Figures 8.3, 8.4 and 8.5.

The following diagrams and text illustrate a UNIX (TM) or UNIX derivative development environment, purely as an example; the theories of categorization and structuring described apply equally to any other operating system environment and programming language and should simply be adapted to your respective ones.

SOFTWARE SOURCES

'Source' must be restricted to pure source code for the deliverable executables, scripts and component configuration files (from which all object files are cleared down before being submitted to configuration control), together with all the build or

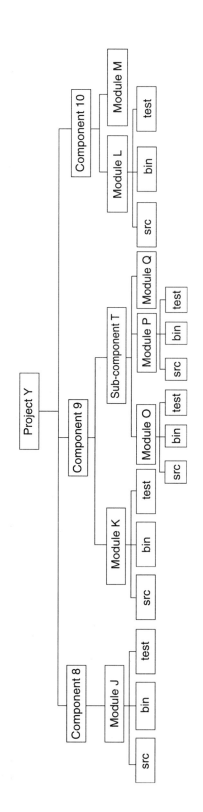

Figure 8.2   Conventional structure for software

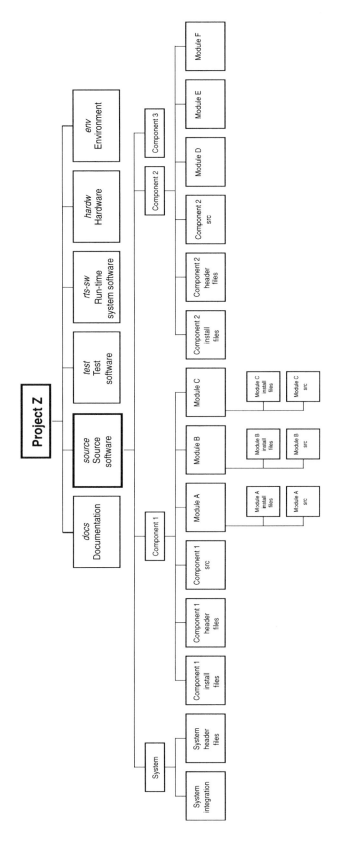

Figure 8.3   Example source software template structures

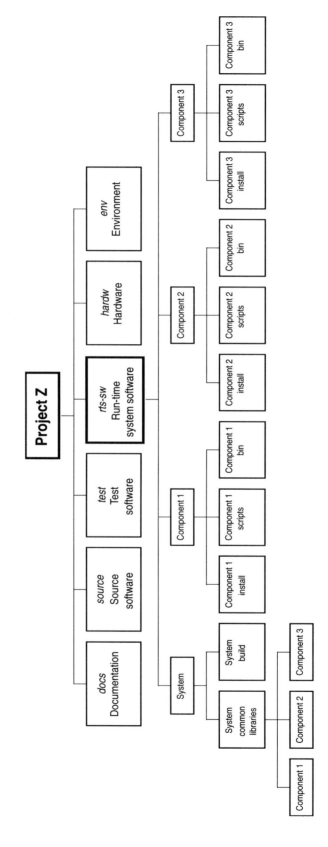

Figure 8.4   Example product or run-time system software template structures

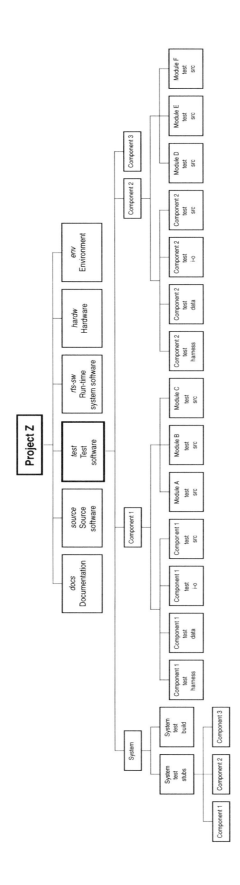

Figure 8.5   Example test software and data template structures

'make' files for every level of module, sub-component and component. These 'make' files must place the resulting executables into the component's structure in the 'product' or 'run-time system' area, *not* back into the component's source area.

SOFTWARE PRODUCT OR RUN-TIME SYSTEM

The resulting executables must, of course, be clearly linked to the source code which created them (see Chapter 9 on how this link may be achieved) so that if errors are found during testing or use, it is obvious exactly which version of source code needs correcting. The 'product' or 'run-time system' area will also need to hold the scripts and data required to integrate the individual component executables into the system whole, plus all shared libraries and system configuration files. It is common practice for this 'run-time system' area to be a flat (e.g. bin) directory but if it is divided into the individual components, as with 'source' and 'test', then it will be possible to avoid a considerable degree of rebuilding following every component-level update.

SOFTWARE TEST

As the name suggests, 'test' must contain not only the test programs or harnesses, but also the test data, test 'make' files and any test stubs, together with scripts for withdrawing the CIs to be tested from the CM database. If a new function is added to a source code module, it is then a simple process to add the matching test steps to the individual test programs or harness and the respective documentation, and to add any extra requisite test data.

This segregation of source code from its test environment and resulting executables offers a number of other advantages. The most obvious is that, with all the source code for a system neatly parcelled as a stand-alone entity, it is a simple process to pass it on to other projects or departments for reuse or adaptation for other requirements or contracts. This approach also simplifies things for object-oriented design.

Yet another advantage is that, for projects where the contract calls for source code to be delivered or put into Escrow (i.e. into the custody of a third party, such as the National Computing Centre, as insurance against supplier failure to support), no post-processing needs to be done to strip off unwanted test or other development files. The segregation also proves beneficial for the developer as, if bugs are found in the code, the withdrawal-for-change and resubmission process of the file, module or entire component is far more streamlined (which can result in crucial time saving with some very 'slow' CM tools) and change traceability is much clearer.

If bugs are found in the source code during integration testing, it may mean that the module or component test programs were also deficient, in that they failed to find the faults earlier. Again, by segregating the source and test CIs and standardizing the structures across all components, clearance of each defect found will be far more efficient. This is because the impact of each defect can be assessed more clearly across the executable's originating source code, the test programs and data, test documentation, all levels of design documentation and, even, the requirements and contractual documentation.

The advantages of this categorization are not just confined to analysis, though, as each defect clearance can be planned and implemented (and audited) individually or together, according to project timescales and workloads. For example, the code will probably need to be corrected immediately, but the corresponding changes to the low-level design document could be added to an existing change request and the design document only updated later. So long as the faults to the document have been clearly identified, actual implementation of the changes can often wait. This will result in an *enormous saving of effort* and is described in more detail in Chapters 9 and 10.

HARDWARE

Obviously no database can hold a terminal, a length of cable or a modem but, as indicated in Chapter 6, these are all CIs. What *can* be held in the database are the inventories describing these and other hardware items, and the information on their respective versions (or 'as built states'). Even a small system will need to track quite a number of hardware items and so, as with software CIs, they need to be carefully categorized and controlled in a hierarchy.

The original system diamond diagram should identify the high-level hardware requirements and then these can be broken down into the lower-level hardware components showing, for example, that a particular installation consists of a console, three workstations, a PC and a laser printer and plotter, on a LAN. Again, by use of simple and logical structure breakdown, defect reporting and clearance can be made much more straightforward, and maintenance stores can even be controlled if stock numbers are included in the information held at each node of the hardware hierarchy. Linked with the hardware CIs should be the respective locations of each type of hardware CI (e.g. Site 1, Site 2) as nodal data. Alternatively, this information can dictate the hierarchy itself, so that it exactly reflects the installation drawings (e.g. Site/Office/User Terminals/Print Facilities), as illustrated in Figure 8.6.

DOCUMENTATION

Documentation structures are very important, but usually totally disregarded even by those projects with good software control. It is essential that the total documentation set

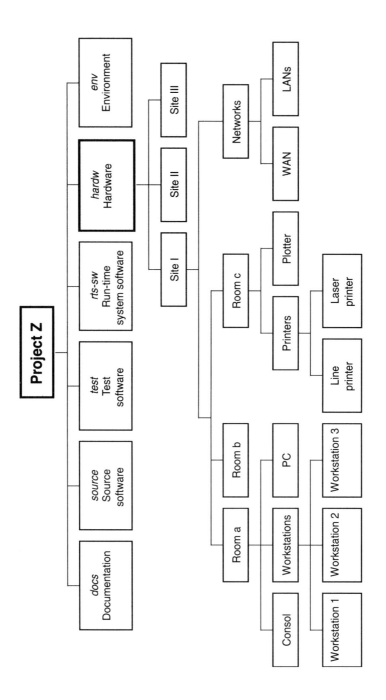

Figure 8.6 Example hardware structures

be categorized into both what affects the system and each component and, like the software and hardware structures discussed above, into type (e.g. requirement, design, test, procedure). Figure 8.7 illustrates a way in which a template structure for the whole system can be created and the nodes then just 'filled in' by the respective development teams, as they produce the documents. Obviously, this structure must reflect the CI plan (mentioned in Chapter 7) and will, in turn, be what is output as the document master configuration index (MCI) (see Appendices A.5 and B).

Different components may need to tailor the template (for example, it may not be appropriate to have a test plan for each module of a particular component as there might be just one plan for several modules), but the point of the overall template is that everyone in the project will know where to find the files and/or information on the document, for any part of the system. This commonality will of course mean that tasks such as impact analysis for changes, identifying the latest issues of any document, and any form of cross-reference between documents and/or the software or hardware that they describe, are very efficient, reliable and easily traceable.

THE ENVIRONMENTS

Another category of CI which, as has been mentioned, often gets missed out is the environment itself, for development, building, testing or using the CIs. Much of the environment can be controlled simply as inventories, e.g. a list of the proprietary software such as operating systems, compilers, packages, or a list of the hardware kit installed, with the respective software versions and hardware serial numbers. This is simple and takes up virtually no space at all, but there are items such as scripts and system or database configuration files that also need to be controlled, together with bespoke communications software and any customization of packaged software, together with any environmental data (e.g. Yellow Pages (TM) user lists, change request status options, help desk response time options, etc., etc.). In other words, the whole environment needs to be planned and controlled in a structured hierarchy, just like any other category of CI.

LINKING CIs

A very powerful and economical way of controlling CIs of any category involves setting up links between them. There are two sorts of links that might be set up— one (the cross-reference) that simply flags that two CIs have an impact on each other, and one (the symbolic link) that actually controls the linked CIs from a single node. Cross-reference links could be used to indicate, for example, that the Component A low-level design document is called up by the Component A high-level design document; that the Module B design document answers Chapter 5 of the Component

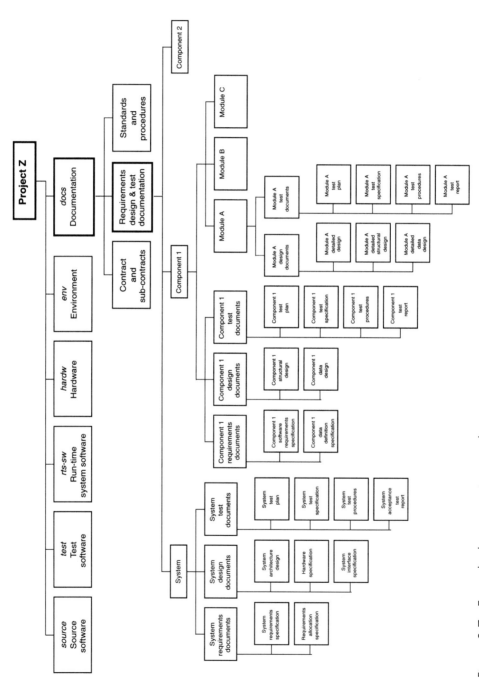

Figure 8.7 Example documentation template structures

HCI specification; or that Volume 2, Section 8 of the requirement specification is what proves compliancy with Clause 90 of the contract. Cross-reference links are informative, but do not actually impact the CI structures themselves.

Symbolic links, on the other hand, actually form structures that 'fool' the user by producing virtual items. For example, three components may all use one of the modules from a fourth component; once the module has been created, the other components could simply take a copy of it and absorb it into their own structures. The problem with this structure, is that there are then *four copies* of the identical software clogging up the system (remember that disc space is always a problem) and, more importantly, it also means that every time the module is changed by the originator, the other three component teams will have to keep track of updates. And what if the other teams forget to make an updated copy, or have altered their original copies (by mistake or deliberately)?

To avoid all these problems, a symbolic link could be set up, as illustrated in Figure 8.8, so that, although the other three components all 'think' they have a copy of the module and can use it and report on it, in fact there is only one copy, which resides under the originating component and which can only be updated by that component team. If the other components want to enhance the module in any way, they must request the 'owner' (through a change request—see Chapter 10) to include their changes in a future update.

A sound CM system will not only provide this mechanism, but will also ensure that the other three components can choose whether to 'stick with' a particular version of the linked module, or to take on board whatever is the latest version, automatically. Another example of the use of symbolic links would be a series of training manuals (for example, for a managing director, the administration, personnel and accounts managers, the accounting staff, the data input clerks and the system engineers supporting the new accounts system). Each of the manuals may have a mixture of common course exercises (e.g. Logging In, Logging Out) and unique course exercises (e.g. Using and Creating a Balance Sheet, Interpreting Error Messages). Just as with the software example using the common module, these training manuals could 'contain' their own unique exercises. For example, only the system engineers' course would need to include the error messages, but symbolic links could be set up to the common exercises so that all could learn how to log in and out. Space would be saved in terms of copies of the soft document files and the technical author writing the commercial manager's course, for example, could not corrupt an exercise in the data input clerk's course. At the same time, however, all courses would be guaranteed to contain the latest version of each applicable exercise.

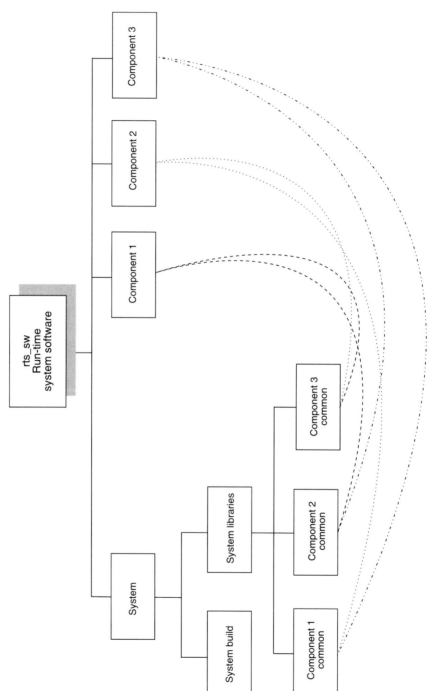

Figure 8.8   Use of symbolic links

MAINTENANCE STRUCTURES

All of this assumes that you have a free hand in how you will structure your CIs. But what about inherited systems that need maintaining, as described in Chapter 4? There will be no choice here as to how the system structure will be formed, since what 'comes over the wall' will be a *fait accompli*, but there is still the necessity to establish exactly what the structure of the maintenance project is and there is still the opportunity to structure the organization's *other* CIs around it. For example, the requirement and design documentation will probably not be structured (and may not even exist!) so that can be controlled along the lines of the applicable nodes in Figure 8.7. And the organization's standards and procedures, the SLA(s) and all the test procedures, programs and data need to be developed and then controlled in sensible structures. Even if the project's system software and hardware have to be treated as a bit of a black box at first (until reverse engineering has worked out what it consists of, as in the example in Chapter 4), there is still the opportunity to change it—if impact analysis proves this to be worthwhile. There is also plenty of scope for structuring and controlling the 'peripheral' documentation and environment CIs.

CONTROLLING THE STRUCTURES

As should be obvious from the above, a lot of work goes into the planning of structures and their creation and it is essential that the structures themselves, not just the CIs in them, be controlled. In the case of symbolically linked CIs, for instance, there should be a mechanism in place to ensure that these are only altered subject to stringent change control—in other words, that the proposed restructures and links are reviewed by everyone affected and that the results are fully checked.

THE SYSTEM SPECIFICATION TREE (SST)

The most unambiguous way of documenting any such structural change, of course, is to mark up a copy of a system specification tree (SST), such as the example illustrated in Figure 8.9. All the *high-level* CI structures should be planned right at the beginning of a project (or as soon as possible, if introducing CM part way through or for maintenance) and then expanded and modified, as necessitated by the evolving design. As the CIs themselves start to be developed and submitted to CM, there needs to be a reporting mechanism so that everyone can see not only where a CI belongs in the structures, but also whether or not it has been created and, if so, what issue or release it has reached.

This information will, of course, be available from the master configuration index (MCI) but, ideally, the information should also be available in graphical format in an SST, which illustrates all the structures for a whole system or even an organization.

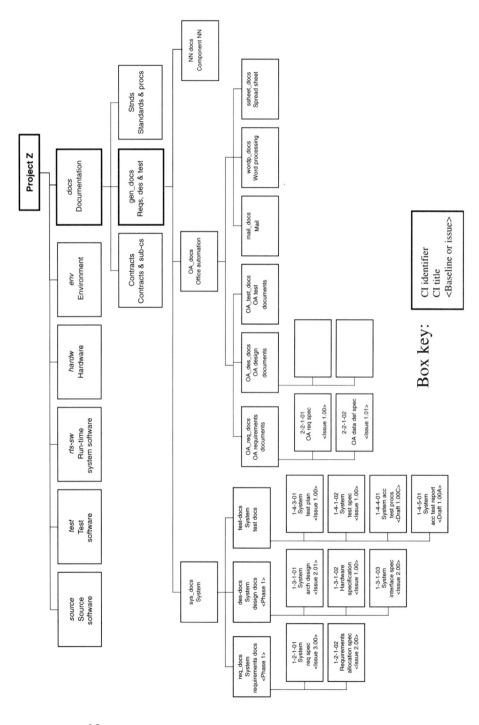

Figure 8.9 Example system specification tree (SST)

The SST could be drawn 'handrolically' if there are not too many CIs but should, preferably, be created automatically from the CM database. The SST will not only give information on the CIs and their respective locations in the hierarchy, but also what mnemonic each CI is known by and its up-to-date issue status, so that the entire configuration under control can be viewed 'at a glance'. There are tools that will illustrate the CI structures on-line but, because most screens or windows are only about 30×30 cm, it is not possible to see a significantly large area of structure at once. The advantage of a printed SST is that it can be marked up and scribbled on with links, resource availability and responsibilities, or whatever is being discussed. If you imagine a team leader trying to explain to a new engineer what modules make up a particular component, for example, the first thing that usually happens is that the team leader sketches a rough logical hierarchy of the component on a scrap of paper, because pictures really are so much easier to comprehend than words. With an SST easily available, the team leader merely has to point out the relevant part(s) of the system configuration.

The SST will also make it easy to see how CIs are grouped so that, as the project rolls through its life cycle, there is scope for *combining* CIs. It is essential to have low-level controls during development but, for maintenance purposes, it may be more efficient to move the level of CI up so that change requests can be actioned at levels appropriate to the project's particular life cycle stage. For example, several low-level software modules (which needed *individual* control during design and development) might be combined into a single higher-level component CI; several individual design documents might be grouped together to form a *set*. Thus, the documents '2-2-1-01' and '2-2-1-02' illustrated in Figure 8.9, which were written and controlled individually during design and development, might be grouped together as the design document set 'OA-req-docs', for maintenance.

[NOTE: Appendix A.4 contains detailed information on CI naming conventions, plus descriptions of the types of nodes that make up an SST.]

SUMMARY

Obviously, the structure templates for any project's software will be dependent on such matters as whether the system is totally bespoke or integrates packaged software, and what operating system(s) and programming languages are employed. The documentation set will be dependent on a company's or project's standards, so the templates illustrated in this chapter should only be taken as rough guides. The point is, though, that planning the CIs and designing, controlling and updating their structures is, actually, as essential to the easy development and ultimate long-term maintainability of a project as designing the system itself!

At the beginning of this chapter, a very simplified way of documenting the flow-down from contract to requirement to system was illustrated in the form of the requirement and implementation diamond, and it was then shown how the diamond could be used to establish the system CI hierarchy. By categorizing all the CIs and controlling them in separate, albeit complementary structures, came the advantages of easy accessibility and conformity, and examples of such structures were given in the numerous figures.

Following on from this, linking was shown to be a useful mechanism for saving space and avoiding some of the problems of variants. Finally, it was shown how important it is to control the structures themselves through use of a system specification tree (SST), not just the CIs, and to be prepared to modify the CI levels as the project moves from design and development through to delivery and maintenance.

9

BASELINING

- – MILESTONES
- – BASELINE TYPES
- – BASELINE PLANNING
- – THE 'V' MODEL
- – DRY RUN TESTING
- – BASELINE 'FREEZES'
- – BASELINE IMPACT
- – BASELINE REPORTS
- – SUMMARY

MILESTONES

Think of a canal, with craft of all sizes motoring, sailing and being paddled along, until they reach a lock. The craft go through the lock independently or, with some large locks, several craft can be let through at the same time. The lock gates have to be opened and the water level carefully raised or lowered, and then the craft move steadily on to the next lock on the canal, closing the lock gates behind them. Now let us give some of the craft names—a group of canoes are named 'Component 1, 2 and 3 Structural and Data Design Documents'; a couple of small motor boats have 'Component 1 and 2 Test Harness and Data' painted on their bows; and two magnificent narrow boats (horse-drawn or with engines, depending on how your imagination is flowing) declare themselves to be 'Component 1 and 2 Source Code'! The lock keys required to fill the locks and move through the gates are document reviews and software tests, and the lock itself is—of course, you have guessed—called 'Baseline A'!

Obviously we cannot carry this metaphor too far because, for a start, real canals have traffic moving in both directions (and projects are difficult enough to manage, without introducing this!); and there is not the same concept of enhancement of real boats whereas, once a CI has passed through one baseline, it is usually enhanced to comply with the additional requirements of the next baseline. But, if you do not try to take it too literally, then the comparison with locks serves well to illustrate that baselines are simply a set of clearly defined targets which the CIs have to get through, success-fully, during the course of the project life cycle.

BASELINE TYPES

What about the canoes in the canal metaphor, though? Is it not only the potential deliverables that are subject to baselines? No—if you accept that a baseline is just a milestone, then each time a document or drawing is issued (regardless of whether or not it is deliverable) or a piece of software is released or development hardware kit installed, a low-level baseline is achieved. High-level baselines are achieved by the accumulation of all the requisite CIs at their respective low-level baseline formal issues.

Look at Figure 9.1, which is an excerpt from the SST in Figure 8.9. There are several documents under the 'system' node, all at various issues (e.g. the system requirements specification is at Issue 3.00) and these have been baselined (or frozen together) at the requirements and design documentation nodes as 'Phase 1', showing that all the requirements and design documents for the system have been written, successfully reviewed and issued. The test documentation hierarchy, however, still has two documents at draft status and so neither the test documentation baseline, nor the overall system-level baseline, can yet be established.

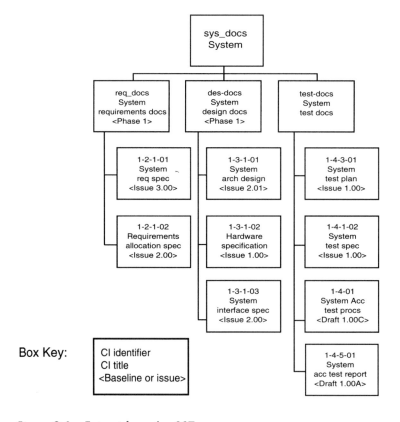

Figure 9.1   Extract from the SST

BASELINE PLANNING

No self-respecting narrow-boater would set off on a canal trip without careful scrutiny of the inland waterways map(s) and without sensible planning of which locks were to be navigated and when. Similarly, all projects should plan not only the delivery baselines, such as 'Requirements Acceptance', 'Phase 1 Code Delivery', 'Overall System Acceptance', etc., but also the internal baselines, such as 'Component 1 Formal Test', 'Phase 1 Integration'. Of course the internal baselines are always planned to a certain extent, but they tend to be treated unilaterally, by the respective component involved, instead of being publicized project-wide. As a result, those involved know what they are working to but, because there is not actually a unique, project-recognized identifier for each baseline, no one else does!

> An example of this caused a hiccough on one project, where a component team had successfully developed their code, submitted it to configuration control with the high-level baseline identifier 'RPT2.01' (i.e. the second formal submission of the 'Reporting' component software, for Phase 2) and passed formal test, all within the planned timescales. The test and acceptance team, meanwhile, had been anxiously awaiting delivery to them of the T&A baseline CI 'EL2.00' (i.e. the first submission of the 'Reporting' software for the second element of formal acceptance testing) and had been wasting a lot of time investigating the CM database and defect report registers for information related to 'EL2.00'. There was actually only one high-level baseline CI (i.e. 'RPT2.01' and 'EL2.00' were the same), but it was being referred to by two completely different names! This did not happen a second time, because the project set up a naming convention for all baseline types and then ensured that each baseline had a unique identifier that was used by all the teams, regardless of whether they were developing the CIs, using them, testing them or delivering them (see Appendix A4.3).

One company had a central filing system where some documents (such as the contract and main deliverables) were classified as 'baseline documents'. Obviously the production and agreement with the customer of these documents established a series of important delivery baselines, but the classification implied that a baseline is a type of CI rather than a *milestone* in the CI's development, review and acceptance life cycle. This is a common misconception and has resulted in some project management and team leaders failing to use baselines as the useful control mechanisms they should be. Even worse, there is a reluctance in many even to mention the word baseline, because they cannot really understand what it means in the context of what they are doing in the project. In software terms, the words 'build' or 'release' are often used instead; this is fine, so long as the teams realize that each successful software build/release is simply the achievement of a baseline.

THE 'V' MODEL

Think of the traditional 'V' model life cycle; it illustrates how every project starts with a requirement, which is then designed and developed, integrated at various levels and, finally, acceptance tested. What the 'V' model then shows is the direct, regressive link that has to be demonstrated between the integrated components and their design and, finally, the full system and its originating requirements. This is solid stuff and has been described and used in many standards, books and projects. It is illustrated, with this book's terminology, in Figure 9.2.

Figure 9.3 shows how configuration management impacts the 'V' model, ensuring that the requisite CIs are lodged with CM prior to the various reviews and tests that establish the high-level 'V' model baselines, and ensuring that all the requisite reports which document each baseline are produced to check and prove its status. By ensuring that all of the requisite CM interfaces and tasks are correctly completed at the right points in the model, demonstration of the regressive link between integration and the design, and the resulting system and its original requirements, is straightforward. It is also clearly traceable and easy to repeat, at any stage and to whatever audience (e.g. project management, auditors and, later, the customer), and it is clear what rework is required, and which versions of which CIs are affected, if the regressive link is not complete.

[NOTE: Obviously, only a sampling of the requisite CM actions could be included in Figure 9.3 as otherwise it would be far too 'busy' to get the required message across.]

DRY RUN TESTING

Some may think it strange that the CIs should be submitted to CM *before* being formally tested but the important word here is 'formally', because one of the keys to the success of any project's development and testing cycle, regardless of whether or not there is a full-blown CM system in place, is '*dry run testing*' of all its software and hardware CIs. What this entails is quite simply that the engineers run through a complete dress rehearsal of the formal test (preferably with their draft CIs in some sort of development control area, as described in Chapter 7), following each step in the test procedure as meticulously as they would if there were a QA inspector or the customer present. If the dry run test fails, the engineers correct the fault(s)—without any CM 'red tape' such as change requests—and repeat the dry run test(s). Only when there is a completed dry run test report (documenting that all the CIs being

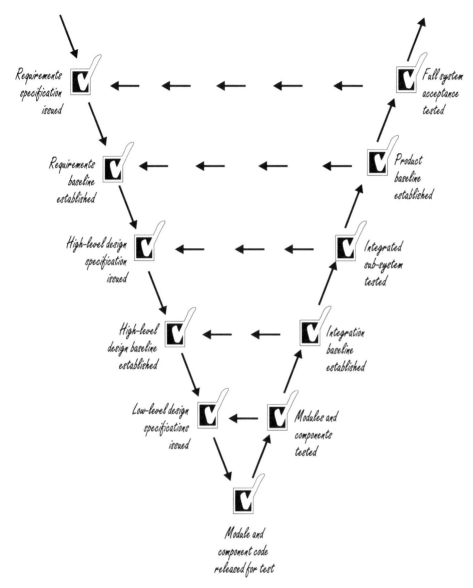

Figure 9.2   The V model

tested are error-free) should the items be submitted to the formal controlled area. The formal tests must take place on CIs withdrawn from the formally controlled area because only in that way can there be indisputable traceability and repeatability. It stands to reason, however, that *if* the dry run tests have been carried out meticulously, then the formal tests will automatically run through quickly and painlessly and there will be no need for rework involving defect reports or change requests. This, therefore, *saves a lot of time* because only a few people and no 'red tape' are involved in dry run

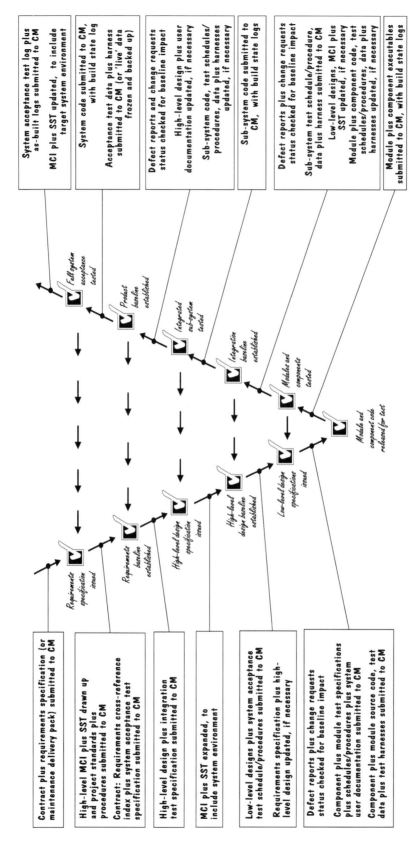

Figure 9.3   The impact of CM on the V model for development and maintenance

tests, whereas formal tests involve QA, CM, project management, possibly the customer and, of course, a multitude of documentation and procedures. Failure at formal tests can *only* happen if the dry run has been carelessly carried out and/or there is a difference in the test environments; the latter may have been unavoidable, but the former is inexcusable and investigation should take place to find out why and how the dry run tests were not done properly.

As described in Chapter 6, establishing exactly (in other words, baselining) what is being formally tested means that there can be much more flexibility in the degree of retesting necessary in the event of a failure. Even if there is not 100 per cent success, the cumulative achievement of the milestone can still be easily measured and demonstrated. But even if a project does not implement dry run testing and, particularly, if there is no development controlled area, the items *must* be submitted to CM *before* a baseline can be achieved. This is so that, on successful completion, the CIs will automatically be subject to all the CM disciplines. It stands to reason that, unless items have been submitted to and withdrawn from CM for formal test, there is absolutely no guarantee that what actually ends up being used is identical to what was tested!

Buckle (1982) devotes a chapter to baselines in his book on *Software Configuration Management*, and one section, which lists the criteria to which all baselines should conform, is quoted here:

- the baselines must be associated with the production of a physical item, either a document or a version of code;
- it is the *acceptance* of this item and not its initial appearance that constitutes the achievement of the baseline;
- acceptance is normally carried out by a review or audit of the item against requirements contained in previous baselines or, in the case of code, the successful completion of testing against previously specified criteria; . . .

BASELINE 'FREEZES'

So, are baselines only useful because they prove that milestones have been reached? No—they do not just prove it, they 'freeze' it, so that the baselined document or drawing (or set of documents or drawings) or the software or hardware module or complete system, can be delivered or used or tested or archived or restored as a single entity, at a known state. One advantage of clearly baselined software or hardware is that it can be reverted to in an emergency. An obvious example of this would be the downgrade of an operating system, following an upgrade which was disastrously incompatible with some application software; or, in hardware terms, the removal of recently installed boards from all PCs in one office, because the new chips were found to be faulty. There is a fine line, in this case, between baselining and backing-up or archiving, but that line is actually quite clear:

- baselining 'freezes' something at a known *state*, while
- backing-up 'freezes' something at a known *time*.

Disc space raised its ugly head in Chapter 5 and baselining can also be used to identify entities that can be held off-line. For example, assume that Phase 1 of a project created a particular environment for the Phase 2 application software to reside on, and then Phase 3 of the project enhanced the original environment for the Phase 4, full system. There might be a period of several weeks when the test and acceptance team need the Phase 1 environment set up, so that they can run formal acceptance tests on the Phase 2 software; at the same time, however, the development teams cannot just sit around idle—they need the Phase 3 environment loaded so that they can carry out informal, integration tests of the Phase 4 code they have nearly completed. Ideally, there would be two test areas so that each operation could be carried out in parallel but this can be costly in hardware and, certainly, disc space and is probably an unnecessary luxury since both teams are unlikely to be using the test area full time. If the Phase 1, 2 and 3 baselined software were stored off-line, then a single test area could be used for both types of testing, with the respective environment baselines being loaded as required.

BASELINE IMPACT

Not only are different baselines of application software likely to be being tested by different teams at the same time, but yet another baseline may be installed at a customer/user site and possibly (albeit undesirably) there may be different baselines at different sites; and that is not taking into account the new baseline that is just being completed by the development teams. And then, of course, the user documentation is different for each delivered application baseline and some, but not all, of the design documentation differs per baseline.... This may sound like a manager's nightmare but, if all the CIs are clearly tagged with (i.e. their CI submission form or record contains a reference to) the particular baseline they impact, then use and control of multiple, concurrent baselines is really not a problem. For example, the test specification and the test report for 'Phase 1 Delivery' might both be tagged with the baseline 'Phase_1'. The respective baseline for every CI might not always be so obvious though. For example, to which baseline would you attach a quality plan, contract or a coding standard? The simple answer is the project's final, overall acceptance, because these documents and many many other CIs lead up to and contribute to the delivery and final acceptance of the entire system—in other words, the ultimate 'lock gate'! So, if in doubt, you could tag a CI with the ultimate project baseline (e.g. 'Sys_Del') but then, as more immediate internal and delivery baselines and their requisite CIs are planned, apply a more appropriate baseline name.

In Chapter 8, CIs were categorized so that they could be structured logically, and it was pointed out that the update of document CIs could be delayed, if time were short, so long as the related software CIs were corrected and re-submitted to the controlled area. But how would anyone know what was related? That is obvious, in terms of CI title or identifier because, for example, a low-level design document should refer to its parent high-level design document and to the component/module name(s) that implement it. But if there have already been several issues of this low-level design document and a couple of releases of the code, then what is the mechanism for establishing that, for example, issue 3.00 of the document describes INT_1.02 of the software? The mechanism is of course baselining and, as described in the next chapter, every CI submission form, defect report and change request should reference not only the issue of a document and/or piece of software which needs update, but also which baseline is impacted.

Baseline (or build) names are an easy way of linking source code with its resulting executables. For example, if several components have been developed and tested and are due for formal integration tests, they should be 'frozen' together at the high-level 'source' CI node with the respective baseline name. Later, when the components have been built together and the resulting run-time system software has been submitted to CM, this high-level 'rts_sw' CI (and the high-level 'test' CI) should be given the identical baseline name. Then, in the future, if a fault is found with the system, it will be clearly traceable *which version of the source code* contained the error and, therefore, needs debugging.

BASELINE REPORTS

CIs need to be controlled and reported on in terms of baseline and this is done through the production of three types of report:

- a master configuration index (MCI), which lists every CI at its latest, formal issue (see Appendix A.5);
- a baseline register, which lists the project's baselines and which issues of CIs achieve it (see Appendix A.6); and
- baseline defect report and change request registers (see Appendices A.7 and A.8).

Let us look more closely at the MCI in Appendix A.5: it is useful to add structural information to the standard index, so that it is clear where each CI resides in the configuration structures, and it is also practical to warn whoever is looking at the MCI which CIs are about to be updated or re-released, in case this impacts their development or delivery baseline. Some quality managers and auditors are unsure of this concept, because they are used to seeing a flat list of CIs with their respective issue status—no more, no less. But is this actually of any use to anyone, if you think *why* they would be looking at an MCI in the first place? For example, a junior software engineer is tasked with coding a module to implement the respective detailed design, according to the project 'C' coding standards, and to submit it for formal test having passed the requisite code reviews and dry run tests, which are documented in the component test procedures. Hopefully, the engineer will know what the latest issue of the detailed design document is, as he or she has probably been involved in its production, but to find out which issues of the standards and procedures have to be complied with, the engineer will have to look up the MCI.

A conventional MCI would indicate, for example, that the component test procedure standard is at issue 1.00, but the poor engineer could waste a lot of time or miss out vital steps in the test preparation if, although the MCI correctly listed the latest formal issue of the procedure standard, it gave no indication that a draft issue 2.00 was just completing review and so the document would be updated within two weeks! If you look at Appendix A.5 in more detail, you will see that some of the CIs have a dual status, i.e. they have entries in both the 'formal' and 'draft' issue columns. The register lists the latest formal issue and, where applicable, an impending update which is currently undergoing review or test. With this fuller information, the engineer can start coding in compliance with issue 1.00 of the procedure standard but with knowledge of the various extra and changed instructions that will become mandatory before the testing is completed. So, the MCI should list all the formal issues of all the CIs and *also warn* of impending updates.

The baseline register (Appendix A.6), however, goes further than that because it groups the various CIs into the respective issues applicable to each baseline, so that their design and development can be easily planned and monitored. The defect and change request baseline registers (see Appendices A.7 and A.8) then carry this forward to ensure that any changes to issued CIs are replanned and monitored in appropriate amendment baselines.

SUMMARY

Looking back through this chapter, we established right at the beginning that a baseline is a *milestone* that has to be achieved or 'ticked off' and the metaphor of a canal lock was used to illustrate the idea of CIs passing through the 'gates' of formal test, review and release, to achieve a given baseline. There are different types of baseline—'high level' and 'low level' (which simply refer to the location in the system hierarchy of the CIs being baselined) and 'delivery' and 'internal' (which are self-explanatory). The importance of planning each and every baseline was emphasized, using naming conventions to ensure that everyone in the project is talking about the same thing.

The 'V' model was used to illustrate traditional high level baselines, and then Figure 9.3 showed the impact of CM on the V model in terms of when CIs should be submitted to formal CM to achieve each baseline. The importance of dry run testing cannot be exaggerated—it may seem to add work but, in fact, it *saves* an enormous amount of procedural paperwork and avoids wasting the time of expensive personnel (because dry runs can be performed by relatively junior engineers, whereas formal tests require the presence of team or even group leaders, QA, CM and test and acceptance).

We saw how baselines can be useful not just in proving achievement but in allowing a particular set of circumstances to be repeated, thus acting as a safety net (like a back-up) and, also, how baselines facilitate the linking of source code and run-time systems and allow flexibility as to what is held on-line. Finally, we established that baselines should be used to plan and monitor the development and release of CIs, using a number of reports such as the master configuration index (MCI) and baseline registers.

In the next chapter, we will see how defect reporting/clearance and change control should also be planned and monitored to ensure that all the right CI 'craft' are corrected and/or enhanced at the right times to queue at the right baseline 'lock gate'! Since we have returned to the metaphoric tow path, remember that one of the most typical features of any British canal is the quaint pub, with landing stage and beer garden, right beside many of the locks. This is not just picturesque and coincidental, it is supremely practical, because after the hard work of opening and closing the gates and steering the craft through, the crew are in serious need of refreshment. This part of the canal metaphor should most definitely be applied to all projects, to ensure that the achievement of baselines is suitably celebrated!

10

ALL CHANGE!

FINDING AND REPORTING DEFECTS

The trouble with achieving a baseline is that, no sooner have you issued the documents or drawings, released the software or installed the hardware for use, then some so-and-so finds something wrong with it! What happens then in many projects is either (a) nothing at all, or (b) the user's individual document or drawing is marked up to correct the mistake, a patch is installed in the copy of the software to which that user has access, or the individual piece of kit is replaced. What is wrong with that? The user's document/drawing is now right, or the software/hardware is working, so what is the problem? The problem is that there are likely to be lots of other users, some of whom will fail to detect the error and so either work to it incorrectly themselves or work on a faulty system or, if they do detect it, will each correct the error in a slightly different way.

The problem is then often exacerbated when the item is updated and not only fails to correct the error (because everyone knew about it but the author!), but is also incompatible with the various uncoordinated edits/fixes/patches/workarounds that have been in use. Even worse, of course, is the fact that because the error was not globally reported, other items produced, which interface to it, are also likely to be defective and will, in turn, be individually edited/patched when they are issued. But in Chapter 4, patches were said to be 'legit' so, like many people hovering around the edges of a CM system, you may now be shrugging your shoulders and thinking that 'you can't win'. But have another look at the end of Chapter 4, because it points out that the essential key to patching is the *immediate* raising of a problem or defect report.

Imagine that an engineer found an error in an HCI specification that had just been issued, e.g. a figure showed a screen which had 'read', 'modify' and 'delete' options displayed. The engineer knows that the delete option should not be displayed on this particular screen and, in our first scenario, would simply cross it out in his/her copy of the document. If, however, a defect report were raised at the same time (and the number of the report marked beside the correction in the document), then not only would the error be removed in the HCI specification when it was updated, but the other engineers responsible for producing the design documentation and code that actually implements the read/modify options would not code in a delete option, in error.

In fact, the term *incident/defect report* (IDR) is preferable, because this allows users to report things that they are not too sure about and which, on investigation, may prove not to be real defects. This does not mean that IDRs should be raised simply to query things like 'How do I print in landscape?' (although, this may imply that the user documentation is wanting), but problems such as 'Following the decision to make the drawings themselves CIs, rather than just the drawings register, the CM Plan and Quality Plan may need amending' are good candidates for IDRs. It will ensure that, in this example, the two plans mentioned will be investigated and updated if necessary, so that 'drop-offs' are avoided. If it is found that neither plan needs amend-ing, then the IDR can simply be cancelled. In the same vein, users/engineers/testers should flag oddities with the system which may not, in some cases, be repeatable but which cannot be explained (e.g. an unexpected abort); if they are unrepeatable, then the IDR might be cancelled but by recognizing 'Unrepeatable' as a defect category and, by investigating all such IDRs together, a pattern may emerge which, in fact, points to a hitherto unsuspected bug.

The secret of getting these incident/defect reports raised is to make them easy to access—whether in paper format or electronic—and simple to fill in. Appendix A.9 lists the most important fields that IDRs should contain, to ensure that the right information is captured and a logical procedure followed. Note that the originator has nine mandatory fields to fill in but, in an electronic system, many of these should be prompted for automatically or created as default entries.

IMPACT BASELINES

So, an IDR has been raised—what now? Should the author of the HCI document update it straightaway, as is implied above? No—because that would mean that some items, with lots of defects, would be updated about 20 times, which would not only cost a fortune in paper, drive the author mad and take up an inordinate amount of review time, but would also make it very difficult to work to, since the baseline 'lock gates' would be continually moving! What *should* happen is that the IDR should be reviewed immediately and a decision taken (preferably by the technical review committee described in Chapter 6) as to its global impact and therefore urgency. Following this, approval to mark up documents or drawings, patch the software, or isolate the defective hardware kit if necessary, or to 'live with' the defect, should be granted. A correction date (i.e. impact baseline) must then be allocated to the IDR, and a change request should be planned that will clear all the IDRs for that particular baseline (see Appendix A.7). With this mechanism, there has been *no delay* in ensuring that the defective item is usable (via patch, mark-up, isolation or workaround), but *everyone is aware* of the defect and, indeed, all other defects affecting that item, which can then be cleared in a single, planned update.

As mentioned in Chapter 6, this makes life much easier not only for the engineers involved, but also for test and acceptance (and, of course, QA). By running an IDR baseline register prior to a formal test, they can see immediately which defects have and have not been cleared on the items to be tested and can then make a decision as to whether to delay formal testing or proceed with these known deficiencies. Long before this, though, these baseline registers will also have offered the team leader an invaluable way of controlling the team's tasks and planning exactly what would go forward for formal test, since defects and enhancements can be worked on in baseline order (e.g. Phase_1, Phase_2), as illustrated in Figure 10.1.

The initial reaction of most project managers, when they find out that lots of IDRs have been raised, is 'this is terrible—we're out of control!' But the irony is that, merely by *knowing* exactly how many defects have been reported, the project is already far more in control than if the faults have been swept under the carpet. And how impressive and reassuring it is to be able to show exactly which issues of every item the defects were on and, then, which issues of each item have cleared, or are planned to clear, them. So actually it does not matter having a large number of IDRs, so long as they are properly investigated and cleared according to plan.

IDR LIFE CYCLE

Let us look, in a bit more procedural detail, at a typical IDR life cycle. The one depicted in Figure 10.2 shows that all IDRs need to be investigated by the developer responsible for the CI which appears to be defective. It may be that the developer agrees with the report and undertakes to correct the defect in a future baseline, by raising a change request on the CI, or by creating a completely new CI. On the other hand, it might be that the user has simply not read the manual properly or has made some sort of

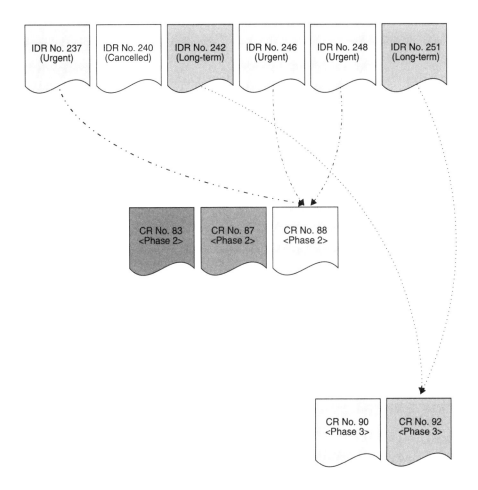

Figure 10.1   Defect reports and change requests planned for clearance,
according to agreed baselines

mistake, so that there is no defect to clear and the IDR needs to be cancelled. Another result of the developer's 'initial investigation' might be that the fault lies with another team (e.g. it had been assumed that it was the software that was defective but the initial investigator believes that the hardware is, in fact, to blame). In this case the IDR should be investigated in more detail and it may be necessary to involve the TRC, QA or some such objective body to resolve responsibility for clearance. For a few IDRs, however, 'detailed investigation' may show that although there really is a defect, it will simply not be possible to fix it, either immediately or perhaps ever. So, in this case, the appropriate concession or production permit procedure will have to be entered into. As shown in Figure 10.1, lots of IDRs can be cleared together by one change request and the investigation of each can, of course, be done in parallel.

TRACKING PROGRESS

So that all this activity can be tracked and controlled (and nothing allowed to slip through the net), it is essential that accurate and up-to-date IDR registers be available (preferably on-line) to all project personnel. It needs to be clear which IDRs are being investigated, which ones are being or have been cleared and when, and which ones look as though they may pose serious problems.

In Figure 10.2 (and, later, in Figure 10.4) you will note that, as each action is completed, the IDR is passed back to configuration control, so that they can check and update its status and progress it to the next procedural step. In other words, configuration control act as the hub of a wheel with the procedural steps radiating from and to the rest of the project, like spokes. This can, of course, be achieved *physically* through the use of paper, but is far better handled *logically* with 'smart' form work flows. In the latter case, the procedural steps can be preset as event triggers, which progress the form through its life cycle, mailing the individuals who need to investigate, implement, close it, etc. Whatever the format—paper or electronic or both—it is essential that configuration control monitor the progression of the forms and the information being added to them, so that the forms can be closed as quickly as possible, with all the required data.

The flowchart in Figure 10.2 shows that there is the possibility of 'external action', which has not been explained. This allows for the inclusion of all sub-contractor deliverables (hardware kit, installation drawings, operating systems, tools, bespoke applications, etc.) and the control of defects in them, through the standard project defect reporting procedure. This means that the true integrity of the *entire* system can be assessed from one database and is a very good way to approach sub-contractor control.

OTHER CONFIGURATION CONTROL FORMS

The most usual action required to clear an IDR is a change to an existing CI and this needs to be controlled through a change request (CR). Firstly, why are CRs separated in this book from IDRs (and the CI submission forms described in Chapter 5), instead of being all in one form, as is the case with many projects? The answer is that it is much easier to track what is happening to each CI—and therefore the overall system—if there are separate forms for submissions (i.e. CI identification), defects and changes. The forms—or at least the information on them—must be held in a database for this to work, though, because trying to trace hundreds of bits of paper or hundreds of soft forms without an easy interrogation mechanism would be totally impractical. As a *minimum*, it should always be possible—whether by using many forms or just one—to state exactly what issue any CI has reached, together with its defect and

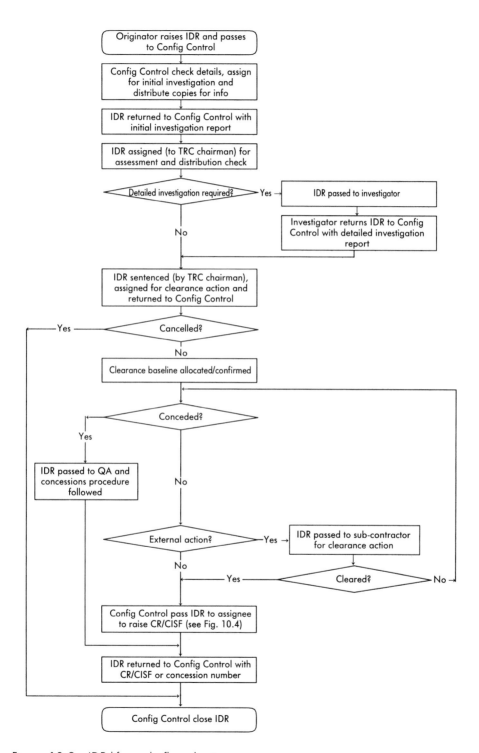

Figure 10.2 IDR life cycle flowchart

change status (e.g. how many uncleared IDRs there are on a particular CI and exactly when and how these will be cleared, and with what updates).

Keeping the IDRs separate (because, eventually, they either have to be cleared, cancelled or conceded), allows individual CRs to be investigated not only in terms of what else will be affected (*technical* impact analysis) but also in terms of such things as whether or not the proposed change is really essential or simply desirable; what the costs in manpower will be if the change is implemented; and whether or not these costs can be passed up to the customer (*total* impact analysis). So, there may be three different forms which affect the submission and re-submission of a CI (see Figure 5.2), but there is a many-to-one relationship between them (i.e. many IDRs may be cleared by one CR, and many CRs by one CI submission form).

THE HELP DESK FUNCTION

Before going on to change control, it is worth mentioning the help desk function, because it is so closely related to incident/defect reporting. It is *not* the same function, though, and should not be fused or confused with it. Yes, the help desk accepts reports on both incidents and defects; yes, the help desk needs to ensure that they are acted on or cancelled. But that is where the similarity ends, because the help desk has *two* interfaces, (a) the customer or user who reports the problems and (b) the developer who investigates and solves them. With incident/defect reporting, however, only the developers are involved, since they are finding, reporting and clearing problems in their own camp—regardless of whether the project is in its maintenance or development phase.

Timing is one of the main reasons that the two functions should be kept separate, because help desk procedures are usually governed by a maintenance contract or SLA, in which *strict response times* for feedback and clearance are established, often including a maximum time or number of 'rings' on the telephone prior to a call being answered! There is nothing so annoying to a customer as being asked to wait on the end of a telephone 'while the screen comes up—it's a bit slow today'! The help desk database and number of users *must* be kept to an absolute minimum so that the customer can be dealt with speedily and efficiently. Incident/defect reporting, on the other hand, although often no less urgent, can be dealt with in a more relaxed fashion. Obviously, as described in Chapter 4, critical problems may require immediate 'fixes' but, as illustrated in Figure 10.3, this is part of the help desk call (HDC) life cycle and triggers, *but does not replace*, a full investigation of the problem, in background mode. This investigation will probably lead to a change in the defective CI(s) which may, or may not, be the same as the temporary 'patch' but which, in any event, will totally overwrite the 'patch' once the update has been formally tested and deemed suitable for 'going live'.

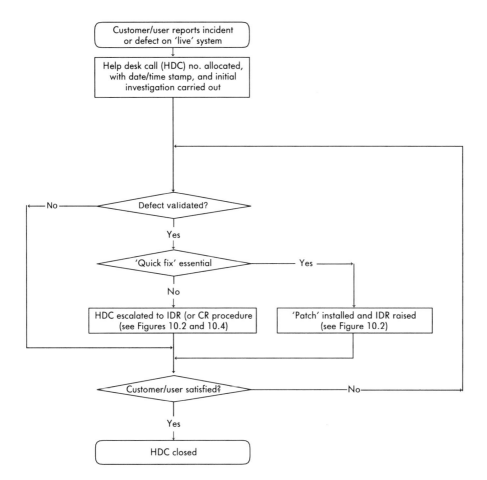

Figure 10.3   Help desk call life cycle

CR LIFE CYCLE

As with the IDRs, it may be useful to look at a typical CR life cycle, as illustrated in Figure 10.4. The first step is for the originator to seek recommendation to raise a CR. This is because much time (and therefore money) can be wasted in investigating how to change a CI, when there is actually little or no advantage to the project in doing so. The mechanism for this initial veto in Ministry of Defence (MoD) projects is through the use of 'engineering change proposals' (ECPs), which then become 'engineering change requests' (ECRs) only if the change is to be progressed.

If the CR progressed in Figure 10.3 is recommended, then the originator must work out exactly what needs to be changed and how (i.e. estimate what tasks need to be done, by what grade of person and how long each will take—see section on impact analysis below). One mechanism for documenting exact proposed changes is to

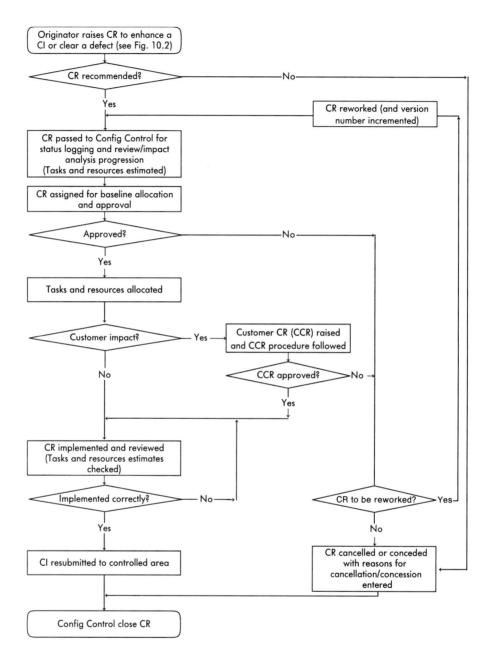

Figure 10.4 CR life cycle flowchart

produce software listings or 'diff' reports proving that the changes proposed to the formal controlled area have worked correctly *under development control*. Alternatively, a clearly marked-up document, drawing or inventory can be attached (in paper or electronic format) to the CR. The CR is then passed via configuration control to the technical review committee (or other suitable review team) for review of the proposed change's technical and commercial merits, i.e. confirmation of the impact analysis details, and allocation of a clearance baseline.

As a result of the reviews and analyses, the TRC chairman will then either reject the CR (for cancellation or rework) or approve its implementation (reported on an 'engineering change notification' (ECN) in MoD terminology). Some changes may require customer approval to proceed and, as the flowchart shows, a customer CR procedural loop, involving the CCB and CCRB discussed in Chapter 6, may have to be followed before the CR can be implemented. Following successful review or test, the CR can be closed (see Appendix A.10).

It is worth noting here that the clearance review/test of a change should include checking not only that the change, the whole change and nothing but the change was implemented, *but also* that the technical and commercial impact analyses were accurate or within agreed tolerances. Where they are not, action should be taken to improve estimating reliability, in other words *process improvement*.

CHANGE IMPACT ANALYSIS

Impact analysis must be carefully carried out because, where technical review does not function properly or is peopled by the wrong level of project personnel, problems can arise.

> For example, one project had a good mechanism for prompting impact analysis on CRs, since all the categories of CI were listed on each CR form and anyone raising or reviewing a CR had to complete a 'Yes/No' entry as to whether any other CIs would need changing if the change in question were to progress. Unfortunately, one section leader consistently failed to flow down information to her teams and, instead of passing the CRs on the requirement document to those 'at the coal face', would enter the impact details herself. As a result, several design documents for one component had to be substantially amended and the code rewritten and tested, resulting in several weeks' slip, because the first view of the *design*-impact changes that this component team saw, was when the high-level requirement document was updated!

Another essential, but often unrecognized, element of impact analysis is establishing *when* a change should take place. We talked about allocating CRs to specific baselines, but sometimes an exact date or even hour has to be agreed (e.g. for the upgrade of an operating system or change in a hardware configuration). In these cases, the CRs should not only explain why the upgrade or change is necessary, and detail or reference applicable release notes, but the proposed *programme* should be detailed as well, so that those reviewing the CR can take it into account in their own plans or, if necessary, veto or delay the upgrade. It stands to reason that it would not be a good idea to upgrade the operating system just before a customer acceptance test, whereas immediately after it would probably be ideal!

CUSTOMER CHANGE CONTROL

One of the most essential uses of change impact analysis is to allow *fixed-price* projects to veto requests for change from the customer. This is vital, because such requests will fall into the following categories (or mixtures of categories) and must be acted on accordingly, i.e. CRs will:

(1) point out genuine errata that must be cleared;
(2) propose enhancements that would improve the system and would be beneficial to the contractor (i.e. supplier);
(3) propose enhancements that would improve the system but would offer no benefit to the contractor;
(4) propose enhancements that would not improve the system but would benefit the contractor;
(5) propose enhancements that would neither improve the system nor benefit the contractor.

Obviously, those requests for change that fall into category (1) must be cleared if at all possible, because failing to do so would result in non-acceptance or concession(s). Category (2) and (4) changes would usually be carried out and at no cost to the customer, but category (3) changes should only be carried out if the customer agrees to foot the bill in terms of manpower and timescales. The customer should be persuaded to withdraw category (5) CRs if at all possible or, alternatively, be informed that the cost of carrying these out will be phenomenal. If the customer still insists, then these category (5) CRs should be treated as extensions to contract.

Compliance with this very simple set of rules is often the difference between succeeding or failing to deliver a contractually compliant system on time and to budget (or satisfying an SLA). It is absolutely essential that this mechanism be built into the project's control system during pre-contract/SLA negotiations and that the customer be made totally aware of it. This may 'hurt' but, in fact, it will work as much in the customer's favour as the contractor's, because the CM system that will be required to implement this control, will give the *customer* much better traceability of how the system is developing and how and when requests for change are being implemented. Above all, it will help to *avoid late delivery*.

IMPLEMENTATION

The actual procedures for requesting changes will, of course, have to include what form(s) is used, how the proposals for change are to be documented, who reviews the CRs and approves them and how the resulting changes are to be proven to be correctly implemented, as mentioned in Chapter 2. This applies not only to internal CRs but to customer CRs as well. (Note: there may be separate forms or the same form used for internal and external interfaces.) One of the most important rules to build into these procedures is that the implementation of any CR (whether for a document, drawing, software or hardware CI) must clear 'the *approved* CR, the *whole approved* CR and *nothing but* the approved CR', so that direct and clear traceability between an update, and the CR(s) that caused it, is *guaranteed*. If further errors are then found during implementation, they can either be worked into the existing CR—which will need to postpone implementation while it is being re-reviewed and re-approved—or be documented on an IDR which can then be worked into a future update.

It is strict compliance with this 'change, the whole change and nothing but the change' rule that avoids costly mistakes like the 'helicopter *and* launching pad' described at the end of Chapter 2. Read that paragraph again and then imagine that the contract had only ever been amended as a result of fully reviewed CRs, which had been approved by both the contractor and the customer. The changes proposed in the CRs should have been very clearly indicated, by being marked up in red ink (or word processor equivalent), so that the reviewers could see the full extent of the proposal. In the case of the helicopter, the 'and' had slipped through because no one had noticed it and this could not have happened if the word had been marked up for insertion and side-barred as illustrated below:

...... helicopter launching pad ......

If technical publications or a secretary had slipped the word in by mistake when *implementing* the CR, there would be no doubt that it was a typing error, and it could simply be removed, because what would have been contractually binding was the *fully signed-up* CR(s), *not* the resulting typed-up document. Indeed, many projects prefer not to update their contracts at all but to work to, for example, 'contract plus approved CRs 001, 003 to 009 and 012'. In this case, an internal *working* copy of the contract should be produced which implements all the approved CRs, for ease of reference only.

One project had an extraordinary amendment procedure which, try as she might, the configuration manager could not persuade them to drop. They had a mixture of three mechanisms for updating their contract, with no hard-and-fast rule as to when any or all of them were to be used and no central review to ensure that the updates were correct!

The mechanisms were:

(1) a fully reviewed and approved contract change request [great];
(2) what they called an 'addendum', which was like a change request but was only reviewed by the commercial manager and the customer. This addendum was sometimes a set of instructions (e.g. 'Delete line 2 of paragraph 3.4 on page 29') and sometimes a typed-up page or set of pages, with or without side-lines [whoops]; and
(3) a mixture of (1) and (2) [help!].

This particular project was the one that suffered the embarrassing, delaying and therefore very costly mistake described as 'clause 33' at the beginning of Chapter 6, which could have been avoided so easily if only mechanism (1) had been used to change that clause, instead of (2). Of course mechanism (1) takes time and therefore money, but this is peanuts in comparison to the *cost of getting it wrong*!

COMMON OMISSIONS

One of the major problems with so many 'change management' systems and, even, current international standards is that for some extraordinary reason they do not include problem or defect reporting as an integral part of configuration control. Yet this chapter (and Chapter 2) has shown just how closely the processes of defect analysis/clearance and change control are linked. Another very common omission, which halves the efficiency of so many CM systems is that, having raised various control forms (such as CRs and IDRs), these are not linked to the *actual* CIs that they are reporting on. What this means is that many projects have carefully proceduralized IDRs and CRs, and carefully controlled CIs, but they report on the two separately, often storing them on entirely different databases! This is hopeless—there has to be a direct, soft link (even if the forms themselves are paper), so that all CIs can be interrogated in terms of the control forms affecting them *and*, conversely, all control forms can be interrogated as to what CIs they impact.

When this sort of CM system was being explained to members of a project who were looking for ways of improving their existing system, they made it quite clear that they thought that the use of a development controlled area, dry run testing and configuration control acting as wheel hubs for forms progression were all 'over the top'. 'We wouldn't have time for that sort of thing', they scoffed. The configuration manager tried to explain the advantages, but could see she was not succeeding and so went on to show them examples of the electronic IDRs and CRs they were then using. On entering the IDR database, she demonstrated how a search could be carried out to find 'all the IDRs ever raised on the project's source code'. The result of the interrogation was '61' and she was about to continue the demonstration by showing how she could carry out further searches on, for example, 'Source code IDRs due for clearance by the Phase_3 baseline', when she was interrupted: 'Do you really mean that there have only been 61 source code IDRs on this enormous project?', 'Yes,' replied the configuration manager, 'and the total number of IDRs raised on *all* our thousands of CIs over a three-year period has only been 352.' The audience were amazed and started comparing the hundreds and hundreds of IDRs their project had already had and the configuration manager was able to point out that 'We have so few IDRs because we make sure that every CI is as "right" as possible *before* it comes to CM. That's *why* we have the development controlled area and dry run testing—so that we don't have to waste time and effort progressing more IDRs or CRs than is absolutely necessary!'

SUMMARY

So, it is obviously very important, first of all, to ensure that the items to be submitted to CM are in a known state and that as soon as any possible defect is found, it is reported—either by the customer or by the internal development teams. The interface for the former should be a related, but *separate*, help desk function which will cope with any necessity for 'quick fixes' and ensure that these are fed into the configuration control system for formal clearance.

All IDRs must be investigated thoroughly and all change requests should be vetted before a lot of work is put into them, to make sure that they are really needed. If they are to be progressed, then full technical and commercial impact analysis must be carried out—not only of all internal but also of customer change requests. Then, equally important is the check (through document/drawing review or software/hardware testing) that the proposed, approved changes have been *accurately analysed and implemented*, so that the originating defects are properly cleared and/or the proposed enhancements are correctly included. The control forms must be linked to the CIs they report on and registers must be produced and analysed regularly to check the status of the forms and the CIs. Above all, procedures must be issued and complied with, to ensure that all this is always done correctly.

This ties in with the previous chapters (particularly the use of the 'development control area' and 'dry run testing' talked about in Chapters 7 and 8), but what the next chapter describes is how to cope with *not* being able to comply with all these rules all of the time!

11

IF YOU'RE GOING TO CHEAT, CHEAT FAIR!

- ONE-OFF SITUATIONS
- MORE INNOCUOUS CHEATS
- THE ADDED VALUE CRITERION
- SUMMARY

ONE-OFF SITUATIONS

'What do we do? We've missed out two changes that should have gone into Issue 1.01—shall we just add them in and hope the customer doesn't notice?' A typical query, which could well have solicited the answer 'Yes', since the document in question was four volumes of 300 pages each! It would be cheating, in a way, but the changes had been approved through a CR, so it was just a technical documentation problem.... The trouble is, that would not be cheating *fair*, because it would result in two sheets, each with 'Issue 1.01' at the top of them, which were *not identical* (i.e. one would have the 'two changes' and the other would not). This is where the troubles could start, because if they got muddled up, or delivered out of sequence, how would anyone know which of the two Issue 1.01s was the *correct* Issue 1.01?

Cheating fair, then, means that nothing must be swept under the carpet; nothing must pretend to be other than it really is or was. Having agreed that all-important principle (and contrary to conventional expectations of a law-abiding and rigidly upright configuration manager), there is no reason why agreed procedures cannot be circumnavigated, when there is genuine need.

Looking again at the query about the two omitted changes, the correct thing for that technical documentation team to do was to implement the changes and update just the sheet(s) affected to Issue 1.02, adding a note at the front of the document (in the 'list of incorporated changes') to point out that the sheet was 'updated to 1.02 due to approved change request NN, omitted from Issue 1.01 in error'. Everyone—from engineer, QA and technical documentation to the customer—then knows exactly what has happened, why and how, and this gives tremendous *confidence* in all other incorporated changes in all the project's documents.

> Let us look at another example of cheating fair: picture a project manager on his knees, hands in supplication (but with tongue in cheek): 'We need to break all the rules, and pretty damned fast!' What had prompted this pantomime was an error in an issued acceptance document which, when signed off by the customer, would result in an extremely large milestone payment. Procedurally, because the document was an issued CI, there should have been a CR raised, reviewed and approved, following which the CI should have been updated and resubmitted to CM for redistribution to everyone on the distribution list. This would have taken a minimum of a day, but the customer was flying out of the country in two hours' time! Obviously they updated the document and got the customer to sign, sans CR *but*, once that valuable payment signature had been obtained, they then raised a *posthumous* CR and wrote on it exactly what had happened and why and, from then on, followed the correct procedures in slow-time. They still had total traceability and a correctly updated, resubmitted and redistributed document, so they had nothing to worry about from an auditor *and* they had achieved the payment milestone!

It is so easy doing things this way, because it emphasizes all the other (99 per cent) occasions when the procedures are strictly adhered to, and it adds credence to the whole concept of CM being 'added value', not 'job's-worth obstruction'. Imagine testing a suite of programs or a set of integrated components; about three quarters of the way through there is a failure that will necessitate changing the code, rebuilding and retesting. A job's-worth configuration or test and acceptance (T&A) manager would insist that this were done before testing continued, but is this really essential? How many times would the test go round the loop if other faults were found in the following test procedure steps?

Firstly, with a good CM system in place, it will be possible to pinpoint exactly what CI(s) are affected by a test failure and the most pragmatic step would be to patch the CIs in the test environment (shock horror—read on!). The test can then be completed with, possibly, even more patches and all the details of all the failures and code changes carefully recorded in the test logs and resulting incident/defect report(s). Using the change control procedures, the CIs that failed the test can then be analysed to see if any other CIs are affected and whether or not the patches installed actually offer the best way of correcting the failure. The CIs will then be amended in the development controlled area, dry run tested for resubmission to the formal controlled area and, if the structures have been carefully thought out (see Chapter 8), only the minimum rebuilding will be needed. T&A can then be called back to pick up formal testing of what had been patched before, without needing excessive regression testing, because CM will be able to prove *which* CIs, and *nothing but* those CIs, have been altered and/or impacted since the first tests.

Don't get this wrong—cheating fair is not advocating avoiding carefully thought out procedures, only occasionally following them in a slightly different order. Sometimes, though, a procedure may not actually dictate the best way of doing things. What do you do then:

(a) rigidly follow the procedure even though you know it is not the best way;
(b) ignore the procedure and do it the way you think is best, but without discussing it or informing anyone; or
(c) cheat fair and, having worked out an improved mechanism, raise an IDR on the procedure to point out what needs changing and to document the fact that it was done this way at this time? As described above, the project can then review the IDR on the procedure, in slow-time, agree or amend the proposal and formally update the procedure so that no one has to cheat at all.

MORE INNOCUOUS CHEATS

The cheats described so far have been 'one-offs', where a conflict in priorities has arisen and, as a result, the configuration manager and applicable project personnel have made a decision either to stick to the standard procedures or to circumnavigate them temporarily and catch up once the panic is over. Because a decision has been required, the cheat has been obvious and the decision to do it a conscious one. The project is in no danger if the cheat-fair rule of documenting what has happened and why is applied.

There are other more innocuous cheats, though, that are really dangerous because they only seem to be fair. Some CM tools embed the CM procedures in the very way in which they work. The tools may enforce the rule, for example, that no item can be placed in the controlled area, without a validated QA approval in the form of an electronic signature. This sounds excellent but, unfortunately, not all the tools allow for the few times when rules have to be broken. A vital flaw with any system that relies entirely on electronic passwords is that they cannot easily allow for the absence of the requisite signatory. What often happens, as a result, is that the signatory's password is just used by someone other than the normal signatory. This sort of cheating is not cheating fair, because it cannot easily be corrected and/or traced. Obviously, there are ways around this problem (e.g. some tools offer 'delegated signatures'), but they need to be carefully thought out and checked. The danger of this type of cheating is that it can be totally *invisible* both to the tool's audit trails and/or to human investigation. In comparison, a paper signature would have 'pp' inserted beside the missing signatory's name.

Another, even worse, example is that very often the people running or interfacing to a CM system think that, because everything is being submitted to and extracted from a CM tool, or because there are lots of signed-off control forms, the project must be totally under control. But, on close scrutiny, those control forms may be found to hold little or no useful information. In a similar vein, simply submitting a CI to a CM controlled area does not guarantee its *integrity*, even if the quality and CM systems governing that submission have worked in checks and controls. Be wary—there might be lots of carefully controlled *rubbish* in your project's controlled area!

THE ADDED VALUE CRITERION

The phrase 'does this offer added value?' can often be used in helping to decide whether or not to cheat fair. The procedures need to 'add value' in the first place (which is, unfortunately, not a forgone conclusion!) and then when a panic—such as the payment milestone documented above—arises, you can ask yourself: 'what genuinely adds more value to the project—to stick scrupulously to the rules or to get this signature and then catch up?' Be careful, though, that you judge the added value as being for the *project*, not just an individual or team, because the latter may be biased.

It is essential for a configuration manager to accommodate these sorts of problems and crises, but it can really only be done by someone who understands hardware and software engineering and project management, as well as quality assurance, and can blend all three together for the optimum good of the project. So remember, when next applying for or offering someone the position of configuration manager—if there is not sufficient technical understanding and management experience, then the CM system will not work and the project will suffer from a too rigid or too lax imposition of controls. As a result, applications for certification to such standards as ISO 9001 will fail—despite all the good advice in the next chapter.

SUMMARY

The concept of cheating fair in CM may have been a surprise and, although this chapter has not been very long, it is in some ways the most important in the book! By slamming the 'that's not in the procedures so it can't be done' configuration manager and introducing the very, very important idea that *anything* can be done if it is really vital to a particular project phase, CM on a project should never be a bottleneck or an obstruction—only an aid. The secret, as you have seen, is to take exact note of what is happening, i.e. how the procedures are being circumnavigated and, in a controlled manner, to bring the process back in line in background mode, without either causing delays and frustrating colleagues or, more importantly, risking an iota of reliability or traceability. Above all, then, what makes the difference between an acceptable, fair cheat and an unacceptable cheat, is the fact that the former is completely and honestly documented and is, therefore, *totally obvious* to anyone tracing what has been done and why. Remember:

Cheating fair means that nothing must be swept under the carpet; nothing must pretend to be other than it really is or was. Having agreed that all-important principle, there is no reason why agreed procedures cannot be circumnavigated, when there is genuine need.

12

BEATING THE BOGEY MEN!

- MINI AUDITS
- REGISTER CHECKING
- FALL-BACK PROCEDURES
- AUDIT-PROOFING
- COSMETIC COMPLIANCY
- THE AUDITORS
- AN AUDIT CHECK LIST
- SUMMARY

You cannot get away from it—audits take up an enormous amount of everyone's time. For at least a week before the ISO auditors come round for their six-monthly check-up, the whole project is running around, destroying old versions of documents, hurriedly raising change requests to clear inaccuracies that they have known about for months, writing job specifications that there was no time to do after the last reorganization, getting project plans up-to-date, etc., etc. Yet that is the daft thing about it—it *has* to be done, because otherwise the project cannot run smoothly and people will not know what they are supposed to be doing and, more obviously, there is a risk of having the ISO certification taken away, so why does no one ever find the time to do these things when they are needed, instead of in desperate preparation for the 'Bogey Men'?

MINI AUDITS

Between 1989 and 1994 a configuration manager designed, set up and managed two CM systems, one for a small company (approximately 120 people, covering four projects) and one for a very large project in a large company (approximately 500 man-years). The configuration manager started with both from scratch and achieved ISO 9001 certification for the CM systems (and the companies) at the first attempts, without ever having a deficiency in the years he managed the systems. One of the secrets of this success was that they built in automatic, regular audits of the CM system, so that while the rest of the company or project were panicking, the CM team just got on with their normal tasks.

You may have noticed in Figures 10.2 and 10.3 that the final step in the life cycle of the IDRs and CRs was 'configuration control close the IDR/CR'. What this means is that the configuration manager must check each form before it can be filed away (or archived, if in soft format), and sign it to verify that all the fields have been correctly completed, that the right people have reviewed/signed the form and that information given in the form is *sensible*. The word 'sensible' is used, rather than correct, because the *correctness* of the information should have been checked during the form's review and implementation by the reviewers and developer/maintainer. The sort of things the 'closure mini audit' is double-checking is:

- If a form has been cancelled by the TRC chairman, has the originator signed his/her agreement?
- If the change request states that it is up-dating a document from issue 2.00 to 2.01, then are both of these issues entered in the appropriate fields and have both issues been lodged in the library?
- If other CIs have been flagged as being impacted by a proposed change that has now been approved and implemented, have CR numbers been allocated and cross-referenced to the other CI changes (or tasks), so that they cannot be forgotten?
- If a CR has been implemented, have all the tasks been signed off and their actual resource allocation been input and compared to the original estimate?
- If an IDR flags a problem in the source code and there is a CR referenced to clear it, has the necessity for another CR (or task) number for the low-level design document and/or test procedure been investigated?

Obviously, all of these and the myriad of other similar potential 'drop-offs' *should* have been correctly completed long before the form is due for closure, but no matter how thorough everyone is and no matter how hard they try, there will always be mistakes. This is often because the reviewers are too tied up in the proposed change or the defect that needs clearing, or because the integrity of reviewers varies widely. It may, of course, be because of the old enemy, lack of time. Having a final check before putting a form 'to bed' is an excellent way of objectively and calmly establishing that when the auditor does the 'pick a form, any form' trick, there will not be any unpleasant surprises. Checking each form does of course take time, but it is *far less costly* than having to rework a CR that has not been properly implemented, or failing an audit.

REGISTER CHECKING

Another relatively painless way of checking that the procedures are being correctly followed and that the CIs reported on really are what they are claimed to be, is to check the master configuration indexes (MCIs) and other major reports, once a month. The most important reports (e.g. the MCIs, contract change registers, customer defect report registers, etc.) should be distributed once a month to the TRC chairman and project manager, as well as being on-line for all project personnel to interrogate. It should be easy to audit the CI and control forms database, by reviewing these major reports before they are distributed, for idiosyncrasies such as 'Are there any CIs with more than two entries in the MCI (i.e. more than the formal and imminent issues described in Chapter 9)? If there are, is this because (a) the database has not been correctly updated or (b) because the CI's owner has not completed a previous submission?'

All the configuration manager has to do is to highlight any report entries that do not quite tie up and then, as a background task, those entries can be investigated. Sometimes there has been a data update mistake, sometimes a form has been incorrectly completed and, sometimes, a procedural step has been left out. Whatever the result, it never takes very long to check and/or rectify, and it is yet another way of ensuring that the CM database is verified and the information about it is dependable. This, in turn, means the 'Bogey Men' *won't get you*!

FALL-BACK PROCEDURES

Of course there is always a bit of special preparation for a formal, external audit, but it should be no more than checking that data input is up-to-date and that there are up-to-date printed copies of the registers and other reports available.

> This stood one configuration manager in good stead at an internal QA audit because, as the auditor walked in, the CM processor went down! Whereas the configuration manager usually delighted in demonstrating everything as an interrogation of the totally comprehensive CM database, he had to run through the entire audit with paper printouts of registers and hardcopies of software, document and hardware/drawing/packaged software inventories, MCIs and SSTs! Actually, it was a very good (and successful) test of the CM system's fall-back procedures, but it certainly made the CM team feel like fish out of water.

AUDIT-PROOFING

STANDARDS

Before any of this, though, there is a simple and essential way of building in audit-proofing. When drafting the CM plan and procedures (or reading through the documentation for an inherited CM system), place a copy of (a) the project's contract(s) or SLA(s) and (b) whatever standard(s) the project/company is required to work to (e.g. internal company standards, BS EN ISO 9001, BS 6488, AQAP 1 and 13, Def Stan 05-57/2, NATO STANAG 4159, American National Standards Institute IEEE 828, etc.) on the desk. Then methodically work through all three sets of documents (i.e. the CM plan/procedures, the contracts/SLAs and the standards), double-checking that they complement each other. For example, in paragraph 4.5.2, ISO 9001 requires that

> Changes to documents shall be reviewed and approved by the same functions/organizations that performed the original review.

This is easy to comply with by, for example, simply ensuring that the CR procedure states that the original reviewers' names or roles must be added to a CR distribution list.

So, look at your project's/company's CM plan and procedures and work out exactly *how* each standard and CM requirement is satisfied. If you cannot find the answer, then it means the CM system needs expanding to include it; if you can find it, then literally tick it off in the standard and the contract/SLA and, preferably, add a chapter or paragraph reference which can be used as an *aide-mémoire* in audits and, also, when training project staff. Some people may think this matching of standards and requirements to the answering CM plan and procedures (or to any other project or company procedures, for that matter) is 'over-the-top', but it is normal practice to cross-reference a contract and its answering functional requirements, so it is surely just as important to do so with the CIs and CM system that give such vital support to the whole project or organization.

EXPLANATIONS AND FURTHER INFORMATION

Beware of expecting to be able to sail through an audit just because you have ticked off what you thought were the requirements in the appropriate standard or contract, though. Most standards are, by their very nature, very high level and in order to satisfy them completely it will usually be necessary to seek out explanatory or lower-level information. For example, in the AQAP series (NATO, 1984), Nos 1 and 13 are far easier to understand if read with No. 14 which explains what they require. When reading paragraph 203 of AQAP 13, for example, it is not easy to understand either exactly what is required for compliance, or its respective applicability to a specific project:

> Provisions shall be made for the periodic and systematic review of the SQC system by the contractor to ensure its effectiveness. Provision shall also be made for evaluation by the QAR who may disapprove the SQC system.

In AQAP 14, however, there are two whole pages of explanation devoted to this paragraph 203, giving guidance on what it is mandatory to include for system reviews, with a list of 'typical questions' that might be asked in an AQAP audit, e.g.:

> 4. Does the contractor take appropriate action when system deficiencies are reported by the QAR? and
> 7. Are review reports made available to the QAR?'

In BS EN ISO 9001 (BSI, 1994), which has now replaced the European Standard EN 29000 and the British Standard BS 5750, references to CM are relatively oblique, and so it is wise to obtain a copy of BS 6488, Code of Practice for Configuration Management of Computer-based Systems (BSI, 1984). This may have been written more than a decade ago, but it still gives good advice on the type of controls and checks that would be needed to satisfy 9001 completely. Reading such lower-level standards and codes of practice can, actually, be very interesting and is certainly beneficial in working out how to design a system in the first place.

Contrary to the beliefs of many, of course, the standards are not there because someone thought it would be a great idea to introduce yet another 'hassle' for the overworked project manager. Running companies and projects according to these standards genuinely improves the working methods and, therefore, the products and the time/costs they take to complete. There is a sting to the tail, though, in that many organizations only comply with the standards just enough to squeeze through the audits and this, actually, *creates work and frustration without giving any of the benefits.*

COSMETIC COMPLIANCY

CM systems fall prey to this 'cosmetic compliancy' most easily and, as a result, have a bad reputation for 'red-tape' administration that adds absolutely no value. Often the mere presence of a CM team makes some people see red! 'Why can't we have scripts written to submit everything to formal control, and why do CM have to track all the forms—surely in this day and age we can set up suitable electronic triggers?' The simple answer to this is that people make mistakes, or sometimes sign blind when under pressure, and a few even deliberately 'hack'. The disorganized ones and the ones who do not like procedures tend to carry out an urgent action more quickly if there is someone standing over them, waiting, than if there is a polite mail message! Also, having an *objective* human interface between the developer and the formal controlled area, just keeping a careful eye on things, weeds out errors. Anyway, the computer facilities themselves can be the cause of errors, as happened not long ago:

> A software configuration controller discovered that although all the right files were being resubmitted, in terms of which ones should have changed for a particular component update, many of the files were zero length! What had happened (and had gone completely untraced by the poor developer re-submitting the files) was that the target processor had run out of space and had simply confirmed each file as it was copied over, without warning the user that the files were being zeroised! In this case, the fact that the software configuration controller was involved as a 'fresh pair of eyes' *saved* a lot of wasted build time.

THE AUDITORS

Audits should be enjoyable—now there is a controversial statement—because if you have set up a CM system to answer the requirements of the appropriate standards and have then checked on a regular basis that the CM team are doing all the things that you agreed were required, there should be nothing to worry about. The auditor's job is to check that a company or project has documented the requisite working practices to ensure that it runs to a specific standard and, then, that it implements those working practices.

Good auditors will ensure that they understand the overall system they are auditing and will approach the audit with a positive, albeit meticulous and firm, attitude because they are there to help the organization improve. A comparison can be made, in this, to speed traps—the aim is to stop people speeding and therefore causing accidents, not to catch them and fine them! Unfortunately, as with any role, there are some short-sighted 'job's worth' auditors, who think that the more unpleasant they are, the more scared the person being audited will be and, therefore, the more likely to make a mistake that can be pounced on and gleefully announced as an observation or even, joy of joys, a deficiency. Ironically, it is the first category of auditor who is far more likely to do a thorough check than the latter, and it is very satisfying to talk to an auditor who really 'knows his or her stuff'.

AN AUDIT CHECK LIST

Demonstrating a good CM system to auditors can also be fun!

> One pair (what is a collective noun for auditors?) had nearly completed their ISO 9001 audit and had said that they were impressed and wanted to know how the configuration manager maintained the obviously high standard. 'Have you got an audit check list' they asked, holding out their own list, '—something like this, perhaps?'. That wonderful scene in Paul Hogan's *Crocodile Dundee* sprang to mind, where a gang of muggers are threatening Mick Dundee with a knife and asking for his wallet. The configuration manager reached into her desk drawer and coolly waved a list much like the one in Appendix A.11 in front of the auditors: '*That's* not an audit check list,' she misquoted, pointing to their list, '*that's* an audit check list!'. Luckily, both auditors had seen *Crocodile Dundee* and laughingly acknowledged the accuracy of her claim. For those of you who do not understand this quote, because you haven't seen the film, it is thoroughly recommended that you rectify this cultural omission by watching the video as soon as possible!

Having a comprehensive but applicable audit check list (the one in Appendix A.11 should be adapted for use on any project), and using it regularly within the CM team, is a sound way of:

- training personnel,
- checking a planned or existing CM system for efficiency and, finally,
- helping to attain zero deficiencies in a formal audit.

SUMMARY

All project management disciplines, including CM, must be governed by some form of standard, with procedures that say how to implement it. Whether the standard is a local one—subject to the approval of a project manager only—or an international one (such as ISO 9001) somebody somewhere sometime must check that the standard is being complied with and the procedures followed. Hence the dreaded audit...*but*, if a CM team follow the guidelines in this chapter, then the audits—whether conducted internally by the configuration manager or QA, or by external auditors—really will be interesting and even enjoyable, instead of dreaded. The worst the 'Bogey Men' will be able to hand out will be the odd minor observation which can be cleared very quickly, but certainly no deficiencies!

So, to summarize, there are three ways of succeeding in audits:

(1) Design everything that the standard(s)/contracts(s) require into the CM system, via its plan and procedures;

(2) Check on a daily/weekly/monthly basis, by conducting 'closure mini audits' on all forms and by reviewing major reports; and

(3) Check regularly with internal informal audits, using an audit check list.

13

CM MEASUREMENT

DATA COLLECTION AND ANALYSIS

There was an old gardener, called Spencer, whose flowers and vegetables were the talk of the whole village. In the pocket of his jacket, Spencer kept a worn notebook in which he jotted down the names of the different brands of runner beans he had planted, the weights of the various types of tomato, the fact that he had experimented with pruning the standard roses three weeks earlier than usual, and pages and pages of other detailed information, painstakingly printed out with the stub of an old pencil he kept behind his ear. Later, over a large mug of tea, he'd ponder the fact that while 'Harpers' Stringless' beans had been all very well for cooking, they had been more difficult to grow than his old favourites 'Dodson's Reliables'; he would certainly try those French tomatoes again, as they had won him a first prize; but he would go back to February pruning for the roses because they had not flowered as well as they should.

Spencer had no patience with modern technology. He never listened to a weather report because he trusted his own knowledge of the clouds and wind direction better than he did the weatherman's. He'd have reckoned things had come to summat if he had been asked to '*collect horticultural metrics*' and come up with a '*revised work plan based on appropriate measurement*'! But that, of course, is just what he had actually been doing for 60 years, and the success of his flowers and vegetables was due quite as much to the meticulous collection of information (metrics) *and* his careful consideration of the results (measurement), as it was to his green fingers.

Spencer's data collection and analysis were not only essential for continued improvement in the gardens he managed, though. The information gathered over the years also ensured that when the old boy finally retired, there was a knowledge base for the new gardener, to help him *maintain* Spencer's high standards and to *build* on them.

Communication is often seriously lacking in the IT industry and when an 'expert' leaves an organization or project chaos reigns, as no one can pick up what the expert has been doing. If, however, the expertise has been collected and stored, and a mechanism has been put in place to ensure that it is continually analysed, then—like Spencer's garden—quality and productivity will not suffer and the whole production process can continue to improve.

A CASE HISTORY MEASUREMENT PROGRAMME

Brameur Ltd's *Starter Kit for Setting Up a Measurement Programme* (Ashley and Team 1994) describes an information system (IS) department case history in which the question 'What do you want from a measurement programme?' was put to an IS management team. The analysed response resulted in the following requirements:

- help in estimating effort and timescales
- help in decision making
- help in improving communications across IS department
- more visibility of the development process
- identifying trends in productivity and effort spent on rework
- identifying where changes are needed
- etc.

From these high-level statements came a clear set of short-term management goals for process improvement which are, in fact, relatively common requirements throughout the IT industry:

- improve the productivity of the development teams
- reduce effort spent on rework
- improve the processes that cause the defects
- reduce the time spent detecting and correcting defects
- improve the effectiveness of system testing
- improve the accuracy of estimates of effort and timescales

Having documented their goals (i.e. 'Where do we want to go?'), the measurement programme had to establish what the current baseline for the organization was (i.e. 'Where are we?') and this was achieved by collecting metrics such as the amount of effort spent on reviews, the number of defects detected at system testing, the number of defects caused by bad fixes. Then came the all-important question: 'How do we get there?', in other words, how would the managers achieve the goals they had set? Finally, there were two more questions that the IS divisional manager wanted answered, so that he could see how well the measurement programme was working, 'Have we got to where we want to go?' and 'How do we compare against the competition?'.

Key performance indicators (KPIs) were associated with each of the goals, as shown in Figure 13.1. [NOTE: Although function points were counted in the indicators in the figure, another measure of system size—such as the number of lines of code (LOC)—could have been used.]

Productivity	Function point count per person month
	Cost per function point count
Quality	Percentage of effort spent on rework
	Percentage of effort spent on reviews
	Effectiveness of reviews
	Effectiveness of system testing
	Average effort in hours to correct a defect found during development
	Percentage of bad fixes during development
Estimates	Variance between estimated and actual effort
	Variance between estimated and actual timescale

Figure 13.1 Key performance indicators from the Brameur Blueprint for Setting up a Measurement Programme

In order to measure a KPI, a set of questions needed to be asked and, for each question, algorithms were defined which would provide the answers, e.g.:

$$\textit{Average effort in hours to correct a defect} = \frac{\text{effort spent correcting defects}}{\text{number of defects corrected}}$$

And from here on it was a straightforward, albeit time-consuming and painstaking, process to collect the relevant data and to analyse it through the established algorithms. The programme did not stop there, though, because there was the IS divisional manager's question of comparison with the competition and its implied goal of beating them. Once the organization knew where it was, where it wanted to go, had worked out how it would get there and *knew when* it had done so, they were able to set specific improvement goals, such as those given below, because they had all the information at their finger tips:

- Within 12 months increase the average productivity of projects by 20%
- Within 6 months decrease the effort spent on rework for the department by 35%

So far, this chapter has sounded more like an extract from a book on metrics and measurement than CM and it is important to realize that, just as CM *cannot* guarantee that CIs are 'fit-for-purpose' but *can* guarantee their safety, availability and traceability, so CM *cannot* guarantee the usefulness of a measurement programme in an organization. What it *can* do, however, is supply much of the data needed for measurement, guaranteeing their safety, availability and traceability. A full CM system will also be able to process that data and present it for analysis in a suitable format. Figure 13.2 models the main processes of a measurement programme (goal setting, data collection, feedback, etc.) and also shows where CM plays its crucial, though limited, part.

So yet another CM discipline is no more than common sense and age-old practice. There is nothing new or mysterious about status accounting and there is nothing clever about CM metrics and measurement; large quantities of data are collected in even a small CM system, almost without trying, and the only clever thing is to work out which of the data are *useful* (and, in an extension to that, what other useful data needs to be collected) and what could be done with it, and then to ensure that it is *used and acted upon*.

EXAMPLE FACTS AND FIGURES

Let us think about some data that is typically collected. 'How many CRs have been raised since project start-up?' is a common one, but it does not actually help anyone very much to know the answer! If, on the other hand, those CRs were categorized and analysed in more detail, with reports on such criteria as 'How many CRs have been raised and/or funded by the customer?', 'How many CRs were cleared within planned timescales?', 'How many resulted in defect reports being raised on the changed CIs?', then the resulting information would be far more useful, since it could be used

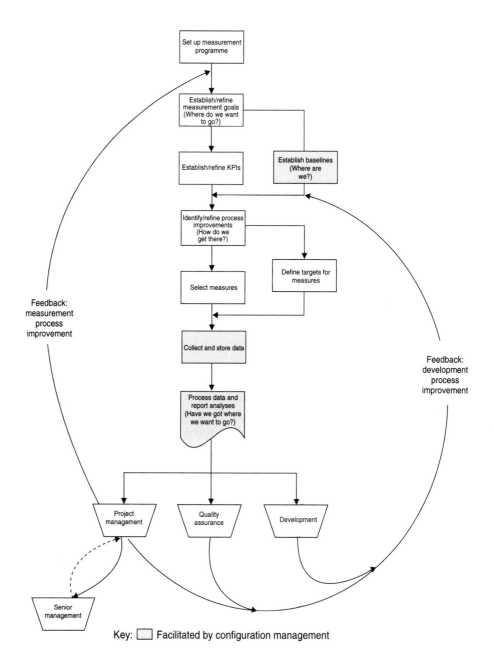

Figure 13.2   CM as part of a measurement programme model

directly for planning and *process improvement*. It is vital, for example, for a project manager to be informed of the numbers and status of changes on the project's requirements, since all approved requirement changes are going to impact directly on budgets, timescales, customer relations, etc.

If the customer is raising lots of CRs, is this because they are unhappy with the delivered system or because they love it and want even more functionality (i.e. are the CRs 'repairs' or 'enhancements'?). If there are a large number of CRs taking longer than planned to clear, then the whole organization (or perhaps only part, if the data has indicated this) may need to be trained better in estimating techniques. If the changes introduced new problems, then the organization is not carrying out impact analysis properly, or is not testing the changes adequately, or both, all of which can be corrected—once identified!

> A configuration manager gave a presentation in London not long ago and one of the audience asked him if he could *prove* that his CM system had saved time or money. The configuration manager had to answer 'No' because, while he and his colleagues knew that it had and that they could not have managed without it, he could not put his finger on any actual statistics that would illustrate conclusively the number of days or months saved by CM in the project life cycle. He had collected quantities of data through the use of 'smart forms', but no one on the project had had the time to analyse them and produce what would have been conclusive evidence.

> Another configuration manager collected data on the large project she worked on and some of the results are listed in Figure 13.3.

SELECTING AND OUTPUTTING THE DATA

The table in Figure 13.3 is actually very difficult to interpret but, if the data is put into a *graph* (Figure 13.4) instead of a *table*, it shows more clearly that there are peaks of activity.

Let us add some more specific information such as the dates of the major delivery baselines:

Phase 1 Requirements Review	Month 14
Phase 2 Requirements Review	Month 24
Phase 3 Requirements Review	Month 28
Build 1 Software Delivery	Month 34
Build 2 Software Delivery	Month 36

Project months	CI submissions	Defect reports	Change requests
1	0	0	0
2	1	0	0
3	2	0	0
4	1	0	0
5	0	0	0
6	1	0	1
7	1	4	1
8	2	6	2
9	3	0	0
10	0	2	0
11	3	8	0
12	0	0	0
13	5	0	5
14	57	4	8
15	12	3	13
16	15	3	19
17	5	0	7
18	2	5	4
19	5	1	11
20	0	1	8
21	2	6	5
22	24	2	14
23	46	17	11
24	70	28	12
25	35	25	24
26	42	25	23
27	68	16	17
28	46	25	26
29	34	36	26
30	36	19	31
31	38	14	27
32	58	18	49
33	70	21	63
34	101	31	74
35	85	32	51
36	131	35	53
37	42	12	43
38	24	9	26

Figure 13.3   Tabular data

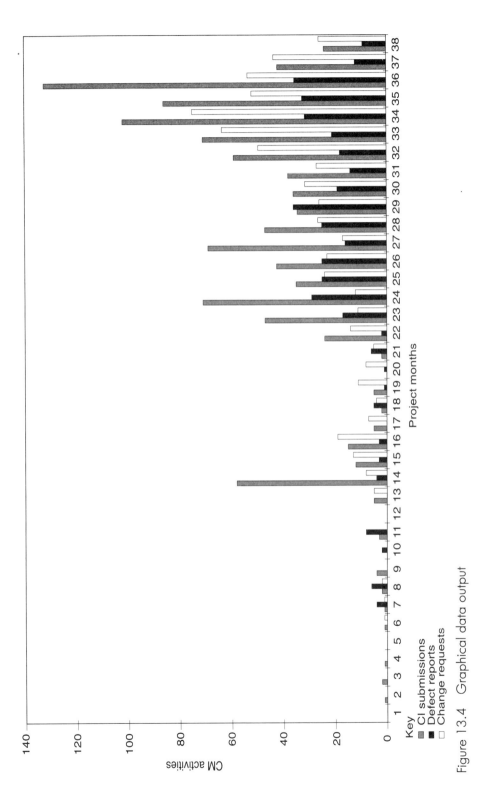

Figure 13.4 Graphical data output

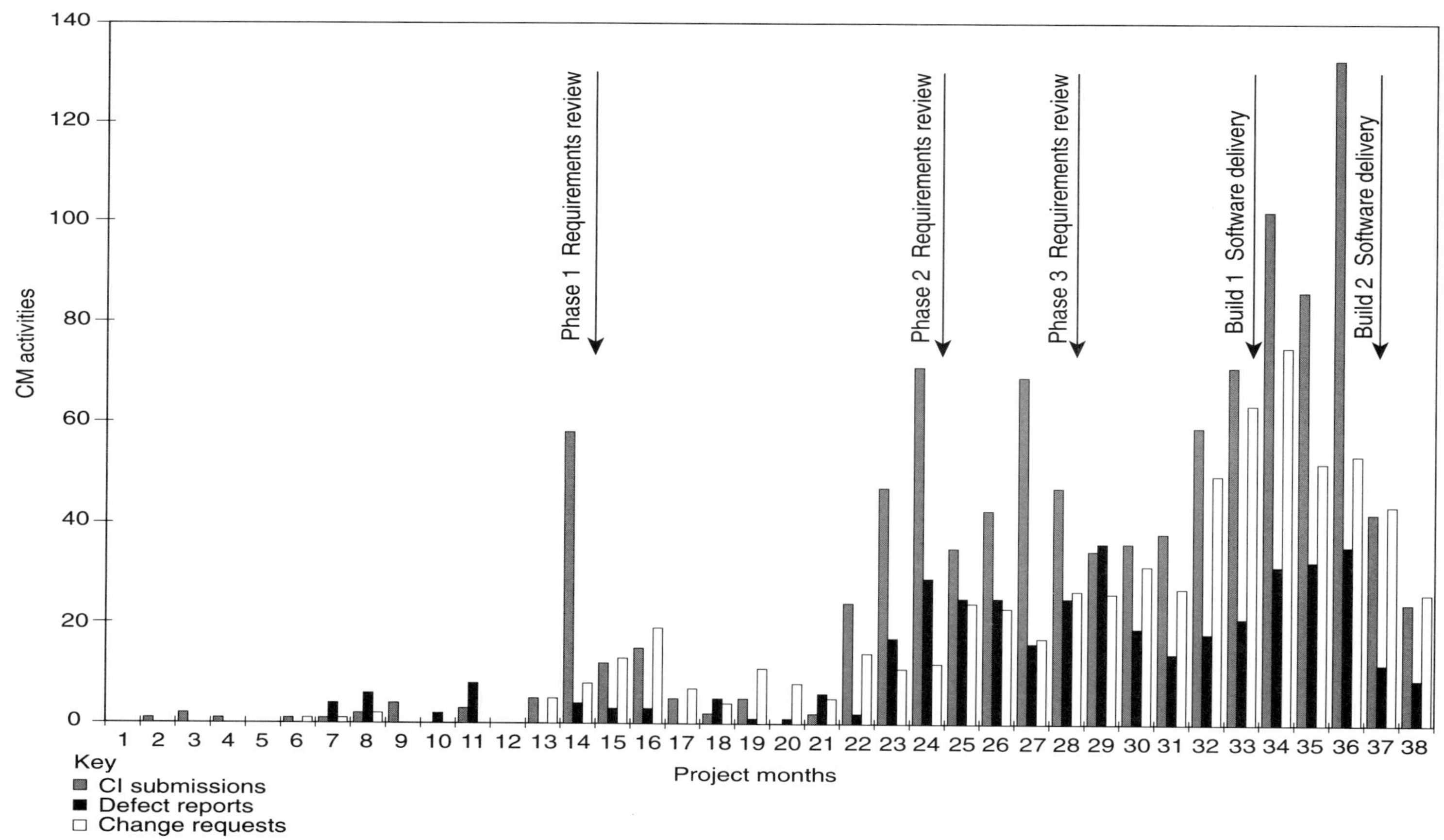

Figure 13.5 Meaningful information

Now the graph (Figure 13.5) is becoming far more interesting, because it shows that there is a great deal of activity just before each major milestone. If we analyse Figure 13.5, it shows something that had not been obvious from the previous two figures, and that is that the project has been suffering from *reactive management*. It has not been coincidence that each milestone has been prefaced with lots of extra work—it has been because of panic! A senior manager looking at Figure 13.5 should be able to use that information to improve his or her project's overall management process. So it is important to remember that you have to ensure that the data collected is not only accurate but is *displayed* in the most appropriate *format(s)* for the intended audience(s). It will probably also be necessary to collect several *types* of data together (such as the 'activity plus the milestones' in the above illustration) in order to get meaningful statistics.

CULTURAL CHANGE

An example of meaningless statistics is the way in which trend analysis is often based on the query 'How many defect reports have been raised?', when defects reported may be of the nature of:

- 'The system doesn't work' (i.e. 500 faults), or
- 'There is a typo in paragraph 4.5.1' (i.e. 1 fault)!

Obviously this is a fatuous example, but it is illustrative of the arbitrary way in which things are sometimes measured. One result of these inaccurate statistics is that engineers dislike raising defect reports on the CIs they use or interface to, and hate defect reports being raised on their own CIs. Far, far better to encourage everyone to raise defect reports, by introducing the culture of '*our* system, or *our team's* CI, has something wrong with it' instead of '*his* CI is wrong', so that all the facts are known, publicized and speedily and correctly cleared. The enormous advantage of flagging all possible defects is that, inevitably, far more are discovered and therefore *cleared* during development, or even the requirements or design phases, rather than during maintenance. This early detection and clearance *saves very large sums of money* since, as stated earlier, the costs of defects found during maintenance have been estimated as around 10 times greater than those found during coding!

Going back to the concept of a culture change in terms of attitude to defect reporting, if engineers know that the CM system is so reliable and the data in it so clearly traceable that defects, once found, will always be traced back to their source, then the temptation to hide defects will be minimized. The CM defect reporting mechanism will, therefore, not only ensure that defects are cleared and traced, but also that engineers will actually take more 'care' over the design and development processes since they know all errors will come back to haunt them, thus reducing the number of defects in the first place! The same, of course, applies to managers and senior analysts involved in the production/amendment of contracts and requirements, etc.

It is important that IDRs (and CRs) are measured in terms of the criticality of each proven defect and the time it takes to clear it, not just their quantity. Another important factor is how often a CI is formally updated. For example, if a piece of software is changed more than, say, three times to correct faults, then it is important to investigate whether this is because its design documentation is below standard, because there is a problem with the actual coding method, and/or because the test procedures are not being kept up-to-date with the CIs they are testing.

PROGRESSION METRICS

All these measurements are being made against actions that *have taken place*, but CM metrics can also be applied to future actions, to help in prioritizing and planning. For example, it is not uncommon for a team leader to have 10 CRs on his/her desk for analysis. All may seem to be as important as each other but, even if the team leader is confident about prioritizing them, his/her values may not be the same as someone else's. Of course, most CRs will have some sort of urgency rating associated with them but, if further metrics are applied which indicate not only the urgency ('priority') of the change but also its importance, e.g. whether it is a major new requirement or just a minor correction to a procedural document ('category'), together with whether or not it impacts the customer ('type'), then a clearer picture will emerge of how speedily a particular CR needs to be progressed.

If the priority, category and type are then given individual values—as shown in the Key of Figure 13.6—then simple addition of all the respective values for an individual CR will result in an indisputable progression rating. These same metrics can then be used, later, to analyse such things as 'Speed of response on all CRs with a progression rating of 0–2' (to prove compliance with SLAs), 'Number of zero rated CRs which resulted in further defects' (to check robustness of emergency procedures), etc.

If a similar classification mechanism is applied to IDRs, then they too will benefit from correct progression prioritization *and* the problem of arbitrary measurement mentioned earlier (i.e. do defect reports cover 1 or 500 faults?) will be resolved.

The CM metrics discussed so far have all been connected with defects and/or changes, but the CM controlled area can store all sorts of information about a project and its configuration, if required. For example, both Chapter 6 and this one have discussed

CHANGE REQUEST PROGRESSION METRICS			
KEY:	PRIORITY	TYPE	CATEGORY
	Immediate = 0 High = 1 Medium = 2 Low = 3	External = 0 Internal = 1	Major = 0 Moderate = 1 Minor = 2
	Progression Classifications		Progression Ratings
Immediate	External	Major	0
Immediate	Internal	Major	1
Immediate	External	Moderate	1
High	External	Major	1
Medium	External	Major	2
High	Internal	Major	2
High	External	Moderate	2
Immediate	Internal	Moderate	2
Immediate	External	Minor	2
Low	External	Major	3
Medium	Internal	Major	3
Medium	External	Moderate	3
High	Internal	Moderate	3
High	External	Minor	3
Immediate	Internal	Minor	3
Low	Internal	Major	4
Low	External	Moderate	4
Medium	Internal	Moderate	4
Medium	External	Minor	4
High	Internal	Minor	4
Low	Internal	Moderate	5
Low	External	Minor	5
Medium	Internal	Minor	5
Low	Internal	Minor	6

Figure 13.6   Change request progression metrics

the inclusion of resources data in CRs, for full impact analysis of a particular change and for use in planning future changes and future projects. That sort of data can be adapted to report the effort required to produce something (i.e. the *input* to an activity). One of the goals of the IS managers in the measurement programme was to 'improve the productivity of the development teams' and they used function point analysis (FPA) to determine the complexity of what was being delivered (i.e. the *output* of an activity). The managers already had the data to determine 'Where are we?' and, having set improvement goals, were able to check 'Have we got to where we want to go?' The managers therefore had the raw materials to achieve their goal of improving productivity, since:

$$Productivity = \frac{\text{output}}{\text{input}}$$

If the right fields are built into IDRs and CRs, the planning department should be able to track what sort of impact defect clearance and changes are having on the project plans, and they should then be able to increase/decrease the timescale contingency for these activities, as was mentioned in Chapter 6. In addition, it is not only a current project that will benefit, because history profiles of existing and completed projects can be used for costing and planning future projects, if the metrics gathered are analysed properly during post development and/or project close-down reviews.

ACTING ON THE INFORMATION

In other words, having collected the information, something should then be done with it, because it does not matter how meaningful the metrics are, they are of absolutely no value unless used. For example, one company set up what was called a 'metrics procedure' in which it was stated that all comments made at a document review had to be categorized in terms of being:

- a 'F'ault, i.e. it would have to be corrected;
- 'N'ot a fault, i.e. the reviewer was wrong;
- a 'R'epetition, i.e. the comment had been made and categorized already;
- and various others.

The Fs, Ns and Rs were useful because they showed clearly what needed and what did not need to be amended and these and all the other metrics were duly noted on the review sheets. But then the procedure dictated that all the numbers had to be totalled per category and then averaged per reviewer. This was a total waste of time because, although the review sheets were carefully retained, no one ever revisited the figures to see if the quality of the reviews could be improved, to check whether enough care was being taken in drafting documents in the first place, etc., so why did the procedure insist that the reviewers go through the time-consuming calculations exercise in the first place?

What this metrics procedure *should* have instigated was an algorithm like the ones in the Brameur Measurement Programme Blueprint, using the review data *plus* defect tracking data to indicate the effectiveness of the whole review strategy:

$$Effectiveness\ of\ reviews = \frac{\text{defects detected}}{\text{defects present}}$$

In other words, there would have been a mechanism for tracing defects that were found later in the development or perhaps even maintenance phase, back to failures in the review process. Improvement of the review process itself, instead of just the correction of the defects, would then have had a downward spiralling effect on the *reduction* of the number of defects found at all. The lesson to be learnt here is:

There is absolutely no point in collecting and reporting on any data, unless it is going to be carefully analysed and acted upon.

The International Organization for Standardization (ISO) has recognized the need to ensure that metrics are not collected 'just for the sake of it', but for a purpose and have introduced an interesting change in the Measurement Standards in the 1994 revision of BS EN ISO 9001. In the original issue, it was recommended that some form of metrics programme be implemented:

> 4.20 Statistical Techniques
>
> Where appropriate, the supplier shall establish procedures for identi-fying adequate statistical techniques required for verifying the acceptability of process capability and product characteristics.

In the 1994 issue, however, the following clause has been introduced to ensure that organizations think about what the *purpose* of metrics gathering is and what they are going to do with the information once they have got it:

> 4.20 Statistical Techniques
>
> 4.20.1 Identification of need
>
> The supplier shall identify *the need for* statistical techniques required for establishing, controlling and verifying process capability and product characteristics.
>
> 4.20.2 Procedures
>
> The supplier shall establish and maintain documented procedures to implement and control the application of the statistical techniques identified in 4.20.1.

SUMMARY

So, metrics gathering and measurement are very practical activities that can be put in place and run without too much extra effort if the will is there and, particularly, if there is a comprehensive CM database to exploit! The measurement programme case history gave examples of the type of data that can be collected and the uses it could be put to and showed how CM can contribute—not by trying to do the whole job, but by providing reliable, repeatable and traceable data to work with. If some extra data is needed, then a good 'smart forms' facility should be able to add appropriate fields to CI submission forms, defect reports or change requests (and/or their associated task sheets) to ensure that the required information is captured. But, having collected the data, effort must be carefully directed so that its manipulation and analysis produce useful information, in an appropriate format.

It may be necessary to go through a re-education process to introduce the culture that it is good, not bad, to discover and report defects and, to do this, global responsibility will have to be accepted in the place of 'finger pointing'. Approaching defect reporting in this way will ensure that the cost of the faults is minimized because they will be reported and cleared earlier and, by correcting not only the defects but also the *process* that allowed the errors to creep in in the first place, then the number of defects that occur at all will be reduced. But CM measurement need not only be connected with defects—all sorts of vital procedural, estimating, planning and general management process information can be gathered and will lead to process improvement if lessons are learnt from the mistakes. Remember:

There is absolutely no point in collecting and reporting on any data, unless it is going to be carefully analysed and acted upon.

14

TOOLS

FOUR CATEGORIES OF TOOL

There are some very exciting things going on in the world of CM tools, the most promising of which is that the industry is now talking about *which* tool to use, rather than whether or not to implement CM and install any tool at all! The tools seem to be falling into four categories, each of which has its own justification for a place in the market, but each of which varies widely in what it has to offer the user. The four categories are:

- version control
- software configuration control
- PC control
- configuration management

VERSION CONTROL TOOLS

By version control tools are meant tools such as SCCS (TM), RCS (TM) and CMS (TM) which:

- perform file versioning for source code and ASCII text, in flat directories, and
- impose fairly basic access controls to safeguard against parallel update of the individual file.

These tools (illustrated simplistically in Figure 14.1) are either installed free with the operating system or cost a minimal amount and, as their low cost and restricted functionality suggest, they usually end up by being enhanced. The engineer needs a

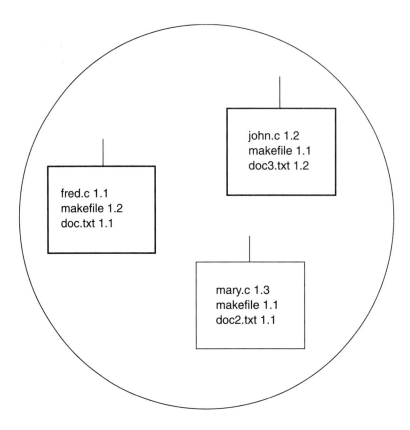

Figure 14.1   What a version control tool offers

more usable system, in terms of the information that can be gleaned about what is being controlled which means, of course, that the tools are not actually *free* but have hidden costs in engineering time and effort.

These version control tools have been available for over a decade, are widely used and pretty reliable and, in the situation where a company genuinely cannot afford more, these tools are certainly much much better than nothing.

SOFTWARE CONFIGURATION CONTROL TOOLS

The second category, the software configuration control tools, is relatively new in the market place and has originated from those engineers who were frustrated with the limitations of the version control tools and have recognized one of the fundamental ironies of configuration management—that by imposing controls, the engineer is given far greater freedom to improvise, experiment or even hack, since the better the electronic controls, the less harm can be done. Many of these tools have also originated from engineers on safety- and security-critical NASA programmes, who *had* to have more sophisticated control. What these tools (see Figure 14.2) add to basic version control is the ability to:

- work in hierarchies, not just flat directories;
- interrogate files in terms of differences between versions; and then to
- be able to merge file variants dynamically.

These software configuration control tools are not limited to performing the basic library functions of deposit, safeguard and release of just source code and ASCII text, either, but:

- offer build control as well (often ensuring that changed files, and only the changed files, are recompiled, through the automatic detection of 'makefile' dependencies);
- offer control over the resulting executable files too; and
- present a far more exciting and inspirational user interface.

Since the tools are designed for the control of developing software in the 1990s, most of them have taken into account the need to interface to CASE tools for requirements traceability and design. Some of the tools do not just interface with each other, but are actually encapsulated, so that it is 'transparent' to the user which of the various functions being performed is being carried out by which tool. The industry has talked about total integration and the emergence of the one, all-singing, all-dancing project management tool, but has not managed to produce it yet; some of these software configuration control tools go a long way towards it, however.

These tools—such as Clearcase (TM), CCC/Harvest (TM) and PVCS (TM)—are the engineers' paradise since they offer tremendous flexibility, with sound control and (although they could certainly be used to control soft copies of procedural documents) are targeted at developing software. Like the version control tools, software configuration control tools allow and indeed encourage further enhancement through scripts, but their drawback is that they, too, suffer from a lack of *project-wide* usefulness. In other words they have no or minimal reporting facilities (status accounting), and the other CM disciplines such as defect reporting, change control or auditing are either completely absent or only available by buying another tool or writing reams of scripts. Nor do these tools try to accommodate any concept of the commercial side of CM, e.g. customer and sub-contractor interfaces or contract control. So there is, once again, a danger of hidden costs in engineering time

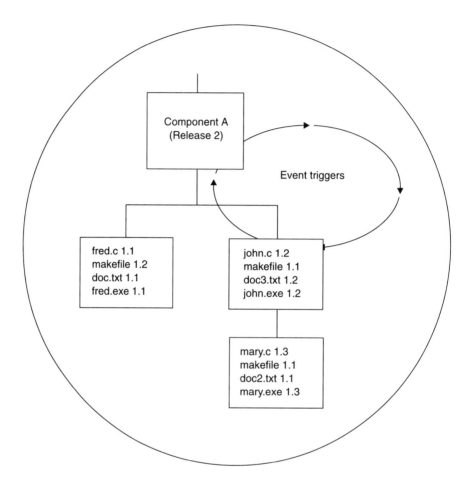

Figure 14.2   What a software configuration control tool offers

to enhance the tools radically and/or to integrate them with several other tools to create a CM 'package'.

PC CONTROL TOOLS

Over the past few years, the quantum leaps in PC software (offering multi-media, object-oriented programming, graphical user interfaces, etc.) and hardware (with the ever-increasing power of PCs and diminishing physical size of notebooks, etc.), has brought with it its own problems in terms of configuration control; even pocket organizers now have greater processing capability than the early PCs! Bad enough that the PCs are moved around from office to office and that all sorts of software can be loaded so easily by anyone, but the problem is exacerbated by the regularly

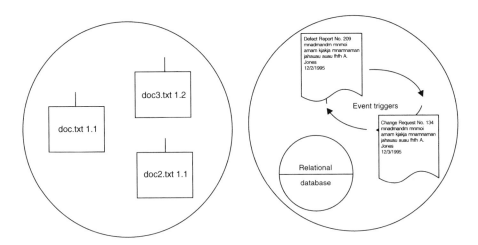

Figure 14.3   What a PC (document, source control, workflow) control tool offers

commuting notebook between the office and home, picking up freeware, games, children's 'A' level notes and home databases en route! The third category therefore encompasses a collection of tools which, although not actually restricted to PCs, have been developed for them, in an attempt to solve these problems.

This category (see Figure 14.3) includes document control, source control and work-flow tools that have emerged as the PC counterpart to mini and mainframe platform control. They all have functionality that nearly does a lot of what is required for total CM and yet none quite achieves it (or at least not on its own). For example, there are some very exciting workflow and groupware packages such as Workflo (TM), Documentum (TM), SmartStream (TM), Red Box (TM), Lotus Forms (TM) and Lotus Notes (TM), which are powerful in that they:

- are able to trigger events and people into action, (so that they could be used for defect reporting, for example),
- can act as a form of electronic library, and
- are attractive and intuitive to set up and use.

The trouble is, they only have token access controls and audit trails and some only control inventories of software and documents, not the files themselves, and so these tools fall seriously short of the mark in a discipline like CM which has its very roots in reliability, repeatability and traceability. Of course the workflow type tools could be procedurally or even electronically linked to software configuration control tools to give more configuration management type functionality, but then you would end up paying for double the licences and double the maintenance, topped up with either engineering or consultancy integration costs as well.

CONFIGURATION MANAGEMENT TOOLS

Ironically, the independence of the PC—which made it so attractive originally—has become recognized as an insupportable threat to organizational control, as the PCs are no longer 'stand alone', but are linked into local and wide area networks (LANs and WANs). CM tools are, therefore, now being developed or ported that treat the PCs as *clients*, linked to and using the power and disc space of, e.g. UNIX (TM) (and derivative) or VMS (TM) *servers*. With this architecture, it no longer matters what is held on the PC itself or whether or not there are good access controls; what matters is that the CM database and vault (i.e. where the *master* CIs, structures and files and all their versions, together with the forms that progress them, are stored) is on a controllable and logically separate platform. Hence the fourth category—the full-blown, fully automated CM tool, as illustrated in Figure 14.4.

The distinction between these tools, such as LIFESPAN (TM), Continuus (TM), CMVision (TM), PCMS (TM), etc., and the other categories is that they:

- encompass all the CM disciplines, so that they do not just provide file versioning and access and build control, but also
- offer easy data collection,
- support defect reporting and change control, and
- can link all these disciplines together in a *single database*. These tools can also
- provide reliable audit trails and report generation, with complete system repeatability and traceability for anyone (from engineer to project manager and customer) to use.

PLANNING AUTOMATION

So, which category of tool should your organization go for? The main difference in why and when each tool could or should be chosen lies in the *approach* to CM of the company or project involved. What is meant by this is that the first to third categories of tool tend to be installed by projects that are aware they have or will have a problem and need to get *something* in place as soon as possible to contain it or, even, which have been instructed to implement CM (without really knowing what that is) and simply go out and purchase the first tool that comes to hand, assuming that this will provide all they need.

The approach to CM, in these cases, is bottom-up which traditionally has the advantages of:

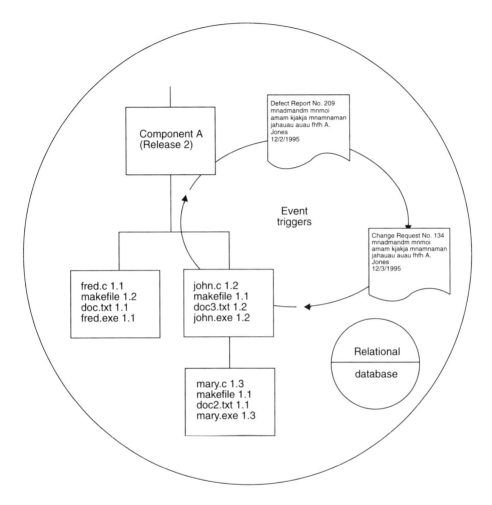

Figure 14.4   What a configuration management tool offers

- being immediately effective and demonstrable;
- involving a minimal amount of planning; and
- requiring lower financial outlay up-front.

This approach, however, also carries with it the obvious disadvantages that are always the result of lack of careful planning. Bottom-up approaches mean that:

- everyone is doing things differently;
- many essential functions will be missed out simply because no one thought of them or thought that someone else was doing them;
- enormous amounts of time and effort will be wasted because the wheel is being invented over and over again;

- clear responsibilities are hard to define and allocate and, therefore, monitor; and
- hidden and unplanned costs can escalate alarmingly.

A top-down approach, on the other hand, will ensure that:

- CM is blended into the other project management disciplines;
- all the customer, standards, management, development and maintenance requirements can be carefully analysed and planned in;
- there are clear lines of communication and responsibility;
- while a lot of effort is required up-front, this can be planned and monitored;
- costs can be carefully analysed and budgeted for;
- interfaces to existing functions and/or standards can be smoothly effected;
- the needs of both management and engineers can be fully investigated and catered for; and, above all,
- the right tool for the job will be more likely to be chosen, because there is a clear idea of exactly what the job is!

Chapter 12 talked about building audit-proofing into a CM system and a top-down approach is essential to enable this to be done. Whatever category of tool you choose, beware of allowing the tail to wag the dog! There are tools that, while they provide support for some or all of the CM disciplines, insist that those disciplines are carried out in the manner dictated by the tool, which actually contradicts many of the advantages of the top-down approach.

TOOLS CHECK LIST

In Appendix A.16, there is a check list of the various attributes of tools that fall into the categories described in this chapter. The findings do not claim to be conclusive or guaranteed—they are just the impressions and information that have been gained through either using the respective tools or from attending vendor demonstrations and reading their documentation.

Some of these tools may no longer exist by the time you read this book; others will have been bought out several times and have different names; the ones that are still around will (hopefully) have gone through several enhancing updates; some may have moved from being version control tools to being software configuration control, or from software configuration control to full CM; and, finally, there will be other tools in the market place which do not even exist at the time of writing. None of this matters—the list is only intended as a rough guide to what the tools provide and is there to *provoke thought* and to act as a guideline for what should be considered and sought when buying a version, software configuration, PC control or configuration management tool.

Take this book with you when attending vendor demonstrations and mark up Appendix A.16 with new tools and the enhanced functionality of existing ones, so that you have your own practical and up-to-date ready-reckoner. You may also find that different tools call the same functions by different names, so be guided by what the function is *doing*, rather than what it is *called* (for example, one tool may talk about 'putting' a CI into the 'CM vault', while another talks about 'submitting' it to a 'controlled area').

None of the functions listed has been weighted—that will be up to you, because each project or company has different priorities—but, once you have established these, the marked-up list will provide invaluable data for tender evaluation and purchase justification and, if done thoroughly, should also underpin the decision to install the correct blend of minimal automated control (i.e. the bottom-up approach) or full CM (the top-down).

QUESTIONS TO ASK ALL VENDORS

There are some functions that all CI control tools—of whatever category—simply have to provide and some questions that must be asked of tools vendors. It is worth going into these in a bit more detail:

- Make sure that the *scope* of the tool is clearly understood by both the vendors and your organization (i.e. which of the four categories does it fall into?). Then make sure that that scope matches your planned approach and budget. If you have decided on a full CM tool, do not let the clever vendor beguile you into thinking a configuration control tool will do it all for you; and, conversely, if you have decided that a version control tool will suffice for your needs, then make sure that you do not pay a lot more for functionality you might not use (although, sometimes, you can get a complete CM tool for the price of one with far less functionality).
- The most fundamental function of any control tool is that it should be able to store files safely and impose *version control*, ideally in a hierarchical structure but, as a minimum, in flat directories. How the tool does this—by storing deltas, inverse-deltas or complete copies—is secondary in consideration to the total reliability of that storage and file versioning.
- Once the individual files are stored, the tool must provide *access control*, so that a file cannot be updated concurrently by accident and so that only the designated users are allowed to read and/or change the files.

- The tool must be *available* when it is needed—this may seem very obvious, but many current vendors are so eager to be state-of-the-art in CM that they are offering functionality in their sales demonstrations that, actually, only exists in the demo prototypes or beta test versions. Not only does this mean that there will be delivery delays once the order is placed, it means, far more seriously, that the tool or its particular enhancement will not have been used in anger and is, therefore, inevitably going to be full of teething problems and bugs, which the vendors will be relying on your organization to help find!

- Ensure that the tool is totally *compatible* with the target operating system(s). Again, this seems obvious, but examples of such problems are that a tool developed for UNIX may not run smoothly on some of the derivatives (such as Sunos or HP-UX (TM)); not all X Emulation software will run under Microsoft Windows (TM); and a CM tool developed for one operating system and then ported to another may have all the same functionality but suffer appalling performance.

- And on *performance*, do not forget that a vendor demonstration will be on a minuscule database of something like five CIs and files, with only one user. The target system's potential size and complexity must be considered, and preferably tested for, as there are some tools currently on the market that work beautifully for small to medium-sized CM systems but grind to a halt and suffer corruption once the database gets too large! Remember that, on average, every formally controlled CI changes about three times and, if the CM system is to control draft CIs as well (as suggested in Chapter 7's 'polo diagram'), then as many as 20 versions of *everything* may need to be allowed for. But do not forget Chapter 7's classification of CIs and non-CIs and ensure that you have a clear idea of exactly what you do and do not want to control.

- *Disc space* has been mentioned many times as causing problems, so the tool should run some sort of delta engine so that only the *differences* between ASCII file versions are saved, not the whole file. Check if and how executables are stored, and whether there is a reliable mechanism for off-lining temporarily unwanted material or deleting 'rubbish'. Can the tool support file compression, or any other space-saving facilities? Tools that have not had to cope with users' disc space problems may never really have been used in anger!

- Give a list to the vendors of all the off-the-shelf tools, that the company or project is or will be using (such as the word processors, desk-top publishers, CASE design and requirements tools, help desk or maintenance tools), and ask them to explain how their configuration control or management tool would *interface* or interact with each. Sometimes full encapsulation may be available—free or at a price. Some tools may have to be recognized as being totally incompatible and, in this case, you will have to decide whether procedural interface as opposed to electronic is sufficient. If vendors say their tools are compatible with others, then ask them to prove it.

- Control of just source or document ASCII files may be quite sufficient for a small project's needs but, if not, then discover exactly how the vendors recommend controlling the other types of CIs, such as drawings, executables, hardcopies, third party software, DATS and discs. Then find out what would be involved in *porting existing configurations* to the tool's vault and/or logging them in the tool's database and, once ported, is it then easy (albeit controlled) to change them?

- Keep in mind the *constraints* that probably apply (such as existing standards and procedures and customer interface requirements) and find out what would be involved in tailoring or enhancing the tool to comply with these constraints. Beware the vendors who imply that this is your problem not theirs, or who assume they can charge large consultancy fees for functions that should be customizable by the purchaser! Remember, the chances of you getting your whole CM system exactly right first time are very small so, if it is difficult to customize the tool, your system is going to be costly not only to set up, but to maintain.

- When analysing the numbers of potential users, think how many need constant access to the CM system and how many are actually only infrequent. Then (except in the case of version control tools), get the vendor to work out the most economical *concurrent user* licence. For example, if you have 50 potential users, of whom only half a dozen would be spending most of each day submitting, withdrawing, freezing CIs and/or raising, monitoring change requests, then a concurrent user licence of 15 (instead of 50) will probably be sufficient and half the price. Check also whether concurrent usage is on a 'per login' or 'per function execution' basis.

- Consider the varying degrees of the users' computer literacy and check that the tool can match their possibly diverse *interface requirements*. For example, if the system is only going to be used by software engineers, then ensure that the tool provides more than just a menu interface; it will need a script (or command line) interface as well. If, on the other hand, there will be 'non-softees' using the system, then check that they will not have to learn reams of complicated and, to them, meaningless syntax to access information, but can be guided through user-friendly menus or 'point and click' graphics. If a remote customer or sub-contractor will need access (either across a WAN, by exchanging DATs/discs or by using paper) then how would the tool control this?

- One of the most important attributes is the tool's *integrity*. Check that it has a documented recovery procedure, preferably coupled with clear audit trails, so that processor and/or tool crashes cause minimal difficulties.

- Finally, do not rely on the vendor's opinion of the tool—ask for a list of at least three current *user reference sites*, preferably ones which are using the tool in the same way your company or project would be using it, and then follow those up. When talking to those referees, do not just ask about the tool, ask about the standard of support the vendors are giving as well. All tools have problems and, now that such a wide variety of functionality is being offered, the level of support given in times of trouble (i.e. friendliness, availability, technical knowledge, location of the tool's source code, consultancy costs, etc.) might be the deciding factor.

COMMERCIAL AND ENVIRONMENTAL REQUIREMENTS

But these are only the requirements for the tool and its vendors! In order to make sure that you get the best CM system, you are going to have to establish your organization's internal environmental and commercial CM requirements. For example, what hardware platform for the CM server would be most compatible with your other systems (if any) and should the user interface be through X terminals or PCs? What is the budget for the software and hardware, and are timescales for the hardware installation, software evaluation, purchase and installation ample? There may be data to port to the new CM system and, when all that is done, people are going to have to learn how to use it, so training requirements have to be established too.

If you are going for the full top-down approach and want to be compliant with ISO 9001, then all these investigations and decisions will have to be documented—possibly in a full operational requirement (OR)—and auditable. But, even for a 'cheap and cheerful' bottom-up solution, almost all of the same questions will have to be asked at some stage, or the solution will not be as cheap or cheerful as you had hoped!

SUMMARY

Some degree of automation is almost certainly essential for CM, even if it is only basic version control of source code to ensure that files are not changed by mistake or changed by the wrong person. Better than that, for the engineers, is to give them a software configuration control tool which will allow them to control hierarchies of any sort of file, to have automated build and file merge facilities and to work in an intuitive development environment instead of one they have had to 'cobble together' for want of anything better.

Alternatively, if most of your organization's CIs are documents rather than software, then a document control tool may be the right answer. The file versioning and access controls are limited but designed towards administrative rather than technical control. If you work or want to work in a proceduralized environment, then a work-flow tool will help enormously, since there is the tremendous advantage of being able to rely on mail messages rather than humans to trigger the user into the progressive actions in a predefined procedure. Decide carefully what your control requirements are and, if they point towards more than just version control, then a software configuration control, document/source control or workflow tool may well be satisfactory. But, since the real cost of the ultimate system is sometimes not much more, it will probably be worth at least looking at what is available in the 'Rolls Royce' section, i.e. the full CM tool solution.

Do not forget that, before buying any tool, a minimum analysis must be made to establish what the *approach* to the CM system design and implementation is going to be; the fable of the tortoise and the hare comes to mind, but that implies that the 'slow but sure' approach is always best—which is not necessarily true. What *is* true is that your organization must go into tortoise mode to think through the approach and only then, if the decision is to go for bottom-up implementation, the hare can take over.

Do not be in such a hurry, though, that you forget the environmental and commercial issues, because otherwise there will be little point in going through the long list of questions on the CM functions, since the tools might not even be able to run properly on the target hardware, software or communications platform!

15

CONCLUSION

You made it! If you have been reading this book in order to get a general idea of *what* CM is all about and *why*, then the preceding chapters will, hopefully, have been sufficient. If, on the other hand, you need to know *how* to set up a CM system, check on an existing one or simply interface to one, then the following appendices should help considerably. Do not be put off if they do not seem to match your particular organization or if they seem 'over the top'—just adapt them, as appropriate, that is what they are there for.

Some—or perhaps lots—of this book will not have been new to you, but did you realize how neatly it all fits together? Had you realized how the four major disciplines of configuration identification, control, status accounting and auditing all break down into the clear-cut functions of planning, library, defect reporting, etc.? so that

---

- *you know what you have got to produce;*
- *once you have got it, you know where it is and what state it is in;*
- *only the right people can use or change it and that they will understand the impact of that change;*
- *useful reports are available;*
- *and the agreed procedures are being followed, so that everything hangs together properly.*

Did you know just where all those different disciplines and functions fitted in to a development project and did you realize how many of them apply equally to maintenance? Hopefully—if you are a manager—you will try to ensure that the right staff are available and able to carry out the requisite CM actions at the right times, or—if you are one of those members of staff—you may have to convince your management how important it is to implement CM, from bid stage right through until the end of maintenance (even if it has be set up through reverse engineering, once a system has been 'thrown over the wall'). It may help to

think of CM as a spinal cord, linking all parts of the nervous system; providing the single channel through which all information can flow, but protecting it with hard and yet flexible vertebrae!

Have you been inspired to take up CM as a career, or make it a worthwhile career for your engineering staff? Make sure everyone in your organization—whether recruiting or being recruited—understands clearly what the roles and responsibilities of the CM team are and, once that is established, make sure that adequate facilities in terms of automation and accommodation are available; the software and document libraries have got to be totally reliable and easy to access, otherwise no one will use them!

It is almost certain that you were able to relate to at least one of the myriad of project interfaces described—from the customer and senior management footing the bills, to the engineers developing and/or maintaining the system(s) and, of course, quality assurance checking that it all runs 'by the book'—and you should now have some useful ammunition to get those interfaces working the way they ought.

Look at the items that you, your team or your project are working on and decide which of them are configuration items (CIs) and, then, what levels of granularity apply in terms of where the CIs belong, because

a configuration item (CI) is any part of the development and/or deliverable system (whether software, hardware, firmware, drawings, inventories and/or documentation) which needs to be independently identified, stored, tested, reviewed, used, changed, delivered and/or maintained. CIs can differ widely in complexity and may contain other CIs in a hierarchy.

But make sure that effort, time and space are not wasted by controlling the wrong things! And, having segregated CIs and non-CIs, make sure that different people are responsible for them and that they use different—and appropriate—levels of control. If the project you are working on is anything but very small, it will probably help to instigate a two-tier CM system, so that you are not clogged up with 'red tape', but can still take advantage of any CM tools and databases installed. Doing this will remove the danger of the 'too much too soon' and 'too little too late' syndromes that plague so many projects.

If you categorize the CIs and then think carefully about the structures, it will be much, much easier to control them. If possible (and if not restricted by inherited project structures), plan to divide the software into 'source' and 'run-time system' and keep all of the test programs, data, harnesses, etc., in yet another hierarchy. Do not forget to plan (or document, if they exist already) the hardware and environment structures and, of course, make sure that all the project's documentation is logically structured so that everyone knows where to look for contracts, requirements and design documents and all the requisite procedures and standards. You may want to impose symbolic or cross-reference links to streamline the use of common items and, because even the smallest project's structure can become quite complicated, make sure that there is some sort of graphical hierarchy diagram (preferably in the form of an automated system specification tree) for everyone to see and use.

Waxing lyrical with the canal scene should have shown you clearly that baselines are something—whether customer imposed or internal—to be achieved and duly celebrated! Baselines (and software builds and releases) need to be planned and referred to with project-wide names, and the traditional 'V' model can help in this, particularly if the respective CM actions are planned in, well in advance, so that everything (having been successfully dry run tested) is safely deposited in the controlled area for formal test and delivery. The beauty of establishing baselines, though, is that they do not just record an achievement, they make a particular version of a particular entity available to whoever needs it, whenever they need it. With the right reports (such as the master configuration index), even the horrors of multiple concurrent baselines can be coped with successfully and relatively painlessly.

Does your organization need a culture change, to make sure that all defects are reported when they are found, rather than swept under the project carpet? And is there—or can you instigate—a sense of global responsibility, instead of the traditional 'finger pointing'? If defects are reported and then cleared early on (in planned baselines), there are tremendous savings in time and resources but, for those problems that do make it through to the delivered system, there should be a related but separate help desk function (which can cope with 'quick fixes') feeding validated calls in to the incident/defect reporting and change control procedures. You know now, if you did not before, that the most important part of processing CRs is *not* their implementation, but the analysis of what impact a proposed change would have on a system, not just in terms of the technical functionality, but also in terms of the timescales and resources needed. For the customer's as well as the contractor's sake, it is important to work out the relative value of each proposed change and, where there is little or no benefit, persuade 'the powers that be' to drop the idea. But, whatever decisions are taken, make sure that they are carefully documented, so that you do not suddenly find yourselves having to deliver a helicopter as well as a launching pad!

And on the subject of careful documentation, the concept of 'cheating fair' may have taken you by surprise . . . almost anything is forgivable if (a) there is genuine added value for the project—not just an individual or team—and (b) every little cheat is fastidiously documented and then rigorously, if belatedly, brought back onto the straight and narrow of the agreed procedures.

Cheating fair, then, means that nothing must be swept under the carpet; nothing must pretend to be other than it really is or was. Having agreed that all-important principle (and contrary to conventional expectations of a law-abiding and rigidly upright configuration manager), there is no reason why agreed procedures cannot be circumnavigated, when there is genuine need.

Even the 'Bogey Men' will not be able to complain if cheating is done 'fairly' because what a good auditor wants to find is a practical CM system, based on applicable company or international standards, where all actions are clearly traceable and all CIs, baselines, tests and deliveries are demonstrably repeatable. The configuration manager should avoid the pre-audit panic by building in not only compliance with the requisite standards, but also 'mini-audits' that check that all configuration control forms have been progressed and closed correctly and that all registers and other reports are both correct themselves and prove that the configurations being controlled are what they are claimed to be. If you are involved in this part of CM, you may find it useful to use an audit check list and, certainly, if you or your organization can confidently 'tick off' all the questions in Appendix A.11, you need have nothing to fear from internal auditors and would almost certainly sail through ISO 9001 certification!

Even if you did all this, though, would you be able to *prove* that your CM system really saves time and effort and, therefore, money? Probably not, unless someone takes the time (or, preferably, is formally tasked) to report on and analyse the data (metrics) collected by the CM system. More importantly, if that data is not analysed (measured) then all the procedural mistakes that are being made will remain undetected and process improvement will not be possible. If you or your organization are not going to improve—through painstaking reaction to carefully collected and analysed information—how will you ever beat the competition?

Finally, it is almost certain that you will need some sort of automation not only to collect and process all the data, but also to relieve individuals of boring and repetitive tasks and to be able to guarantee the state of your CIs. Validated, electronic controls and procedures are far more reliable than those carried out by even the most conscientious of people. But make sure that you get the right tool for the job and that you actually know what 'the job' is going to be—whether through bottom-up or top-down systems analysis. When buying a tool, use the check list in Appendix A.16 and bombard the vendors with questions that will ensure that all your CM (and commercial and environmental) requirements are met.

Whether you will be running a CM system, interfacing to one or just paying for it, do not be put off by mistakes from the past or by other people's lack of knowledge of what CM really is:

> 'The trouble is our project manager doesn't like CM very much,' confided a test and acceptance manager, 'come to think of it, he doesn't like testing much either!'

CM has been misunderstood and badly managed on many projects, sometimes with inadequate facilities and poorly trained personnel. But it is not the only project discipline with problems and, reassuringly, it is now being recognized as vital by individuals, organizations and standards bodies alike, so that its ability to help both development and maintenance projects will escalate, as the IT industry accepts this long-overdue change in configuration management's image.

APPENDIX A

TEMPLATE SOLUTIONS

Appendix A consists of a series of independent sections giving examples of career paths and job descriptions, configuration control forms, procedures, check lists and status accounting reports. These are called 'template solutions' because they should be adaptable by any project to suite complexity, size and/or duration, regardless of what point in the project life cycle the solutions are being introduced.

Appendix A.1 offers solutions to the problem raised in Chapters 2 and 5, i.e. that there are currently no career paths or standard job descriptions for configuration managers or controllers, although the British Computer Society (BCS) plans to include CM in its updated Industry Structure Model (ISM3). The experience requirements and the career paths documented in Appendix A.1 can be adapted by any company's human resources department and applied to its organization's career structures.

Appendices A.2, 3, 9, 10 and 14 give details of the fields that should be included in a project's configuration control forms. One of the purposes of these appendix templates is to make you, the reader, think carefully about what sort of data you need to collect, in what format, and to think what you actually want to do with that data—huge reports that nobody reads or understands do nothing to enhance project efficiency, whereas reports giving information that is wanted, understood and acted upon is what CM status accounting is all about. These five appendices are in table format and give details of each field that the forms could or should contain. Attributes for each field such as whether or not it should be searchable (i.e. for data collection in a report or register), a description of the type of entries and, finally, an indication of the respective project personnel responsible for the fields' completion and/or validation, are also included.

Appendix A.4 offers ideas for naming conventions which could be used for documentation, software, baselines, configuration structures and the control forms—your organization or project may well have standards for these already, in which case all you have to do is build them into your CM system. If any of the conventions is missing, however, it is strongly advised that you set one up and ensure that it is followed, as naming conventions are one of the simplest and yet most effective methods of communication.

Appendices A.5, 6, 7, 8 and 15 are examples of the various reports and registers that should be used and acted upon by all project members—they show how important it is to include the right fields in the control forms and how simple it should be to use the data, collected in the control forms, effectively. The layout of any report (and whether it is produced electronically or in paper format) is unimportant; what matters is that it must be meaningful and useful to your organization.

Appendix A.11 is the audit check list for use when designing a new CM system, when evaluating an existing one, and/or keeping an existing one on the straight and narrow. The list should, of course, be used for formal audits but it will probably be even more useful if used as an *aide-mémoire* for the sort of procedural controls and conventions that need to be set in place and/or checked regularly.

Appendix A.12 gives guidelines as to the sort of topics that should be discussed in a technical review committee (TRC) meeting, a configuration control board (CCB) and a customer configuration review board (CCRB). This assumes that there is one or more fixed-price contract/SLA with an external customer; where the customer is internal, the terms of reference for the CCB and CCRB may well be combined and the agendas amalgamated.

Appendix A.13 documents the topics that should be covered in a project's or organization's CM plan. It assumes that lower-level procedures will be written and, therefore, concentrates on *what* needs to be done, not *how*.

Finally, Appendix A.16 offers the reader information on existing control and CM tools and an easy way to evaluate new and updated tools, in the form of a tools functions check list which, as stated in Chapter 14, should be actively used and kept up-to-date.

APPENDIX A.1   CM CAREER PATHS AND JOB DESCRIPTIONS FOR CONFIGURATION MANAGERS AND CONTROLLERS
(DRAFT INPUT TO THE BRITISH COMPUTER SOCIETY INDUSTRY STRUCTURE MODEL)

[INSERT INTO BCS ISM2 APPENDIX C2]

CORE STREAM: INFORMATION SYSTEMS POLICY AND MANAGEMENT

	Sub-Stream Name	**Sub-Stream Name**	Sub-Stream Name	**Sub-Stream Name**
Level Number	**Strategy & Planning Specialism**	**Internal Quality Specialism**	Configuration Management Specialism	**Consultant Analysis**
0				
1				
2			IM CM2	**IM CA2**
3		**IM Q3**	IM CM3	**IM CA3**
4		**IM Q4**	IM CM4	**IM CA4**
5		**IM Q5**	IM CM5	
6	**IM P6**	**IM Q6**	IM CM6	
7	**IM P7**	**IM Q7**	IM CM7	
8	**IM P8**	**IM Q8**	IM CM8	

KEY: **Existing BCS ISM(2) in bold**
Draft Insert not in bold

SUB STREAM DEFINITION: Configuration Management Specialism

SUB STREAM REF: IM CM

The function of management of information system configurations, in terms of their identification, control (including storage, access, problem reporting and change control), status accounting and auditing, often against acknowledged external criteria (such as the ISO 9000 series) and of providing expertise in the application of configuration management techniques to all stages of the information system life cycle, assuring the application of such techniques and procedures wherever appropriate.

Level Number	Sub-stream Name	Job Title
	Configuration Management Specialism	
0		
1		
2	IM CM2	Junior Config Controller
3	IM CM3	Configuration Controller
4	IM CM4	Configuration Controller
5	IM CM5	Configuration Manager
6	IM CM6	Configuration Manager
7	IM CM7	CM Consultant
8	IM CM8	CM Consultant
9		

[Note: Examples of Level 6 (Configuration Manager) and Level 2 (Junior Configuration Controller) Models follow]

STREAM Core: Information Systems Policy and Management

SUB-STREAM: Configuration Management Specialism

LEVEL: 6   CELL REF   IM CM6

JOB TITLE: 'CONFIGURATION MANAGER'

RECOMMENDED ACADEMIC BACKGROUND

Preferably educated to degree level. As an alternative, GCE 'A' level (or equivalent) entrants with previous experience in Technical or Development streams of the ISM, or with IS conversion training following a period of non-IS work, will also qualify. At this level, length and quality of experience as demonstrated by achievement can compensate for lack of formal education.

EXPERIENCE AND LEVEL OF SKILL AT ENTRY

(A) EXPERIENCE

(1) EITHER at least two years' satisfactory performance at Level Five in the Configuration Management Specialism sub-stream, OR a minimum of eight years with at least two years at Level Five gained in other streams of the ISM which include involvement with Configuration Management, OR at least eight years' exposure to a commercial/administrative/industrial working environment which must include a minimum of three years' direct IS experience as a user as well as direct experience of the application of quality and Configuration Management to projects or products of a complex nature.

(2) Must have demonstrated successful leadership of a team of technical staff and have demonstrated competence in project leadership tasks.

(3) Must have demonstrated good working knowledge of the employing (or a similar) organisation's policy framework, management structures and reporting procedures for the Configuration Management environment and evidence of practical involvement in all stages of the information system life cycle, from feasibility through post-implementation and support.

(4) Must possess a wide and up-to-date knowledge of hardware and software in general, with at least three years' practical experience of the software development life-cycle including a working knowledge of project management, feasibility,

analysis, design, coding, testing, implementation and maintenance of complex software systems.

(5) Must have experience in applying the relevant technical and procedural standards constituting a Configuration Management system.

(B) ATTRIBUTES

(1) There must be demonstrable evidence of mature inter-personal skills and adaptability, with the ability to handle constructively contact with the most senior and junior levels of employing organisation and/or customer and/or sub-contractor staff.

(2) There must be demonstrable evidence of advanced technical problem-solving ability, through successful completion of periods of responsibility, handling issues of complexity within the software sector. This must be coupled with above average attention to detail, skills of observation and persistence and meticulous operation.

(3) The ability to influence through persuasive argument in the context of both informal and formal meetings must be evident.

(4) Exhibition of judgement and maturity in assessing the need for strict standards/procedural compliance, taking into account the real project requirements as well as any external considerations.

(5) Must be fully conversant with and be able to interpret relevant National, European and International Configuration Management and Quality standards.

TASKS

(1) Evaluation of existing Configuration Management systems and the design and implementation of new/improved systems.

(2) Design and application of requisite Configuration Management requirement(s), plan(s) and procedure(s).

(3) Enhancement of proprietary tools, where applicable, to produce an effective Configuration Management environment in terms of database, transactions and report generation.

(4) Determination and documentation of Configuration Management requirements for any sub-contractors and the review and audit of resulting sub-contractor Configuration Management systems.

(5) Training, or operating a training programme for, all levels of staff on the general principles of Configuration Management and its precise application in the employing organisation.

(6) Presentation of the principles of Configuration Management to customers and/or sub-contractors and liaison with these organisations in all matters relating to Configuration Management.

(7) Briefing and direction of subordinate staff, the monitoring and assessment of quality of performance of all work within scope of responsibility and the fostering of positive attitudes to quality.

(8) Estimating and planning the work of a team or project group within agreed policies using any appropriate planning tools, and producing plans to standards required. Must be able to participate in long term planning for warranty/maintenance configuration support.

(9) Monitoring and reporting on progress against plan according to standards, and handling exceptions referred from below relating to schedules, working methods, resources, staff matters or technical difficulties. Only those decisions clearly outside scope should be passed upwards, with proposed solutions whenever appropriate.

(10) Conducting technical interviews/assessments for recruitment/selection and ensuring that staff are developed appropriately to the benefit of the organisation and the individual concerned.

(11) Within a controlled structure, take responsibility for a team or teams of technical staff involved in carrying out the following tasks:

    (a) Determination, maintenance and documentation of configuration structures and items, in conjunction with other relevant technical authorities, and controlling the issue or release of configuration items for test, development use and/or delivery to customer.

    (b) Control and documentation of proposed changes to all configuration structures and items and the management of re-releases of changed items.

    (c) Defect reporting documentation, investigation and clearance.

    (d) Design and maintenance of a document reference library.

TRAINING AND DEVELOPMENT REQUIRED

(1) Should receive continuing training as needed in management skills in preparation for accepting further responsibility for activities within the overall breadth of configuration, quality and project management.

(2) Should keep up-to-date an overview knowledge of all aspects of IS that impact Configuration Management, particularly in relation to aids to productivity and service quality, by reading, attending relevant seminars and courses and by interaction with colleagues.

(3) Should receive broad management and business training to establish a better understanding of the environment of senior management, including risk management,

safety and security related issues, finance and commercial, marketing and legal issues.

(4) Should be seen to be acting professionally at all times and encouraging professional standards amongst subordinate staff.

(5) Should be seen to be active professionally externally to employing organisation by, for example, involvement in national/international standards committees.

STREAM Core: Information Systems Policy and Management

SUB-STREAM: Configuration Management Specialism

LEVEL: 2   CELL REF   IM CM2

JOB TITLE: 'Junior Configuration Controller'

RECOMMENDED ACADEMIC BACKGROUND

Preferably educated to degree level. As an alternative, GCE 'A' level (or equivalent) entrants with previous experience in ISM, or with IS conversion training following a period of non-IS work, will also qualify. More mature entrants with longer periods of relevant IS experience and lower educational levels may qualify.

EXPERIENCE AND LEVEL OF SKILL AT ENTRY

(A) EXPERIENCE

(1) At least one year's satisfactory performance at Level One in any sub-stream of the ISM stream.

(B) ATTRIBUTES

(1) Planning/scheduling own work competently.
(2) Meticulous method of working and attention to detail.
(3) Interest in and general awareness of all phases of the project life cycle.
(4) Must show aptitude for becoming effective and persuasive in the presentation of Configuration Management concepts and local procedures, both orally and in writing.

TASKS

(1) Under supervision, the maintenance and documentation of configuration structures and items and controlling the issue or release of configuration items.
(2) Under supervision, the control and documentation of proposed changes to all configuration structures and items and the control of re-releases of changed items.

(3) Under supervision, defect reporting documentation and maintenance.

(4) Under supervision, the maintenance of a document reference library.

(5) The use of requisite operating system(s), hardware and tool(s) to maintain the Configuration Management system.

(6) Familiarization with the concepts of Configuration Management and increased awareness of quality and project management disciplines, over all phases of the project life cycle.

TRAINING AND DEVELOPMENT REQUIRED

(1) Should receive formal training in the overall concepts of Configuration Management and specific local standards and procedures. Such training should be given or approved by the senior Configuration Management function.

(2) Through reading and observation, coupled with formal training if appropriate, should widen knowledge of the overall information systems life cycle, through all its stages, and Configuration Management's applicability to each stage.

(3) Should receive training in oral/written communication skills.

(4) Should receive any relevant training in the specific Configuration Management tool(s) and/or their software and hardware environment.

APPENDIX A.2   CI SUBMISSION FORM (CISF) FIELDS

Table A2.1   CI Submission Form (CISF) Fields

Field name	Attributes	Description	Completed/ amended by
CISF security classification	Mandatory (in classified projects), validated, searchable and fixed format	Entries such as 'Unclassified', 'Restricted', 'Commercial-in-Confidence', etc. (Note: This refers to the classification of the CI submission form, *not* the CI itself)	CI owner
Sheet n of n	Mandatory and fixed format	Not only the respective sheet number, but also the total number of sheets including all attachments, if any	CI owner
CISF no	Mandatory, validated, searchable and fixed format	A unique, sequential number, preferably allocated by a CM tool but could be from a log book. (Note: This could equate to a unique CI ID number plus its Issue number, if only Documents, Drawings and/or Inventories were being controlled)	Configuration control (or CM tool)
CISF status	Mandatory, validated, searchable and fixed format	Dependent on the exact procedure being followed, will contain options such as 'Draft', 'Implementing', 'Awaiting_Hardcopy', 'Awaiting_Files', 'Cancelled', 'Cleared', etc., to describe what is happening to the CISF	Configuration control
Actionee	Mandatory, searchable and fixed format	The name (or user account for electronic CM systems) of the person currently carrying out the actions described in the status field	Configuration control
Status date	Mandatory, validated, searchable and fixed format	The date on which the status changed (or the CISF was raised if status = 'Draft')	Configuration control
Action due date	Mandatory, validated, searchable and fixed format	The date by which the action described in the status field must be completed by the actionee and the CISF returned (or mailed) to CM or the next actionee	Configuration control
CISF source	Mandatory, validated, searchable and free text	Either 'First Submission' or a cross-reference to the CR which necessitated the re-submission of the CI	CI owner
CI project	Mandatory, validated, searchable and fixed format	The name of the project for which the CI is being submitted. (If only one project is being controlled, then the project name should be set by an automatic default)	CI owner

Table A2.1   (continued)

Field name	Attributes	Description	Completed/ amended by
CI ID and title	Mandatory, validated, searchable and fixed format	The unique identifier e.g. '1-3-1-01' and title e.g. 'System Architecture Design' of the CI being submitted, and its exact path in the SST	CI owner
CI issue/ release number	Mandatory, validated, searchable and fixed format	The unique, new issue status of the CI being submitted, e.g. 'Issue 2.01'	CI owner
CI baseline	Mandatory, validated, searchable and fixed format	The name of the baseline to which this particular issue of the CI is linked, e.g. a customer delivery	CI owner's line manager
CI classification	Mandatory (in classified projects), validated, searchable and fixed format	The security classification of the CI itself, e.g. 'Unclassified', 'Restricted', 'Commercial-in-Confidence', etc.	CI owner
CI type	Mandatory, validated, searchable and fixed format	One of 'Software', 'Documentation', 'Hardware Inventory', 'Drawing', etc., describing the CI	CI owner
CI destination	Mandatory, validated, searchable and fixed format	Information with regard to whether the CI will be used strictly within the project or will be delivered to sub-contractor(s) and/or customer, e.g. 'Internal' or 'Deliverable'	CI owner and line manager
CI distribution	Mandatory, searchable and free text	List of people and/or locations to whom the CI has been formally distributed, in paper and/or electronic format. May include a document copy no, if applicable	Configuration control
Test/review references	Mandatory and fixed format	Reference to an identifiable test or review which proves that the CI is of sufficiently high quality to be submitted to the formal controlled area, together with the date of the test/review and the name of the person responsible for it	CI owner's line manager
Known deficiencies	Mandatory and free text	Either 'None' or a description of known bugs or 'drop-offs', e.g. 'Chapter IV tbd', 'Mail Menu contains stubs only', etc.	CI owner
Resulting or associated IDRs	Mandatory, validated, searchable and fixed format	'n/a' if there are no declared known deficiencies, or reference to an IDR(s) which fully documents the deficiency and which will, therefore, ensure that it is cleared in a subsequent submission	CI owner

Table A2.1   (continued)

Field name	Attributes	Description	Completed/ amended by
Links	Optional and fixed format	Details of links (cross-reference or symbolic) to other CI(s), if any	CI owner
Soft file info	Mandatory and free text	Details of the location of the CI's soft files (in the development controlled area, a directory and/or a tape or diskette), and a list of all the new, unchanged, updated and deleted files that make up the CI to be submitted (this should be obtainable automatically, from a CM tool)	CI owner
CI owner details	Mandatory, searchable and fixed format	The name and dated signature (ink or electronic) of the person submitting the CI	CI owner
Line manager details	Mandatory and fixed format	The name and dated signature (ink or electronic) of the person approving the overall quality of the submission	CI owner's line manager
Submission confirmation	Mandatory (unless CISF cancelled) and fixed format	The name and dated signature of the configuration controller who effected the submission of the CI into the formal controlled area	Configuration control
CISF closure	Mandatory, validated, searchable and fixed format	Dated signature proving that the 'Closure Mini Audit' has been satisfactory	Configuration manager

APPENDIX A.3   CI WITHDRAWAL FORM (CIWF) FIELDS

Table A3.1   CI Withdrawal Form (CIWF) Fields

Field name	Attributes	Description	Completed/ amended by
CIWF security classification	Mandatory (in classified projects), validated, searchable and fixed format	Entries such as 'Unclassified', 'Restricted', 'Commercial-in-Confidence', etc. (Note: This refers to the classification of the CI withdrawal form, not the CI being requested)	Borrower
CIWF no	Mandatory, validated, searchable and fixed format	A unique, sequential number preferably allocated by a CM tool, but could be from a log book	Configuration control (or CM tool)
CIWF status	Mandatory, validated, searchable and fixed format	Dependent on the exact procedure being followed, will contain options such as 'Draft', 'Processing', 'Hardcopy-on-Loan', 'Cancelled', 'Cleared', etc., to describe what is happening to the CIWF	Configuration control
Actionee	Mandatory, searchable and fixed format	The name (or user account for electronic CM systems) of the person currently carrying out the actions described in the status field	Configuration control
Status date	Mandatory, validated, searchable and fixed format	The date on which the status changed (or the CIWF was raised if Status = 'Draft')	Configuration control
Action due date	Mandatory, validated, searchable and fixed format	The date by which the action described in the status field must be completed by the actionee, e.g. a document returned to the library	Configuration control
CI project	Mandatory, validated, searchable and fixed format	The name of the project to which the CI belongs. (If only one project is being controlled, then the project name should be set by an automatic default)	Borrower
CI ID and title	Mandatory, validated, searchable and fixed format	The unique identifier e.g. '1-3-1-01' and title e.g. 'System Architecture Design' of the CI being requested, and its exact path in the SST, once known	Borrower and configuration control
CI issue/ release number	Mandatory, validated, searchable and fixed format	The unique, new issue status of the CI being requested, e.g. 'Issue 2.01' if known or 'Latest Formal Iss/Rel'	Borrower and configuration control
CI classification	Mandatory (in classified projects), validated, searchable and fixed format	The security classification of the CI requested, e.g. 'Unclassified', 'Restricted', 'Commercial-in-Confidence', etc., once known	Borrower and configuration control

Table A3.1 (continued)

Field name	Attributes	Description	Completed/ amended by
CI type	Mandatory, validated, searchable and fixed format	One of 'Software', 'Documentation', 'Hardware Inventory', 'Drawing', etc., describing the requested CI	Borrower
Transfer medium	Mandatory, validated, searchable and fixed format	A description of the medium on which the borrower requires the CI, e.g. 'Hardcopy', 'Disc', 'DAT', 'LAN', etc.	Borrower
Reason for request	Mandatory and free format	A reference to an IDR, CR, minutes, or correspondence, or a description of why the borrower needs the CI	Borrower
Borrower details	Mandatory, searchable and fixed format	The name, position and dated signature (ink or electronic) of the person requesting access to, or the loan of, the CI	Borrower
Authorizer	Mandatory (dependent on the organization) and fixed format	The name, position and dated signature (ink or electronic) of the person authorizing the access to or loan of the CI	Authorizer
Transfer details	Mandatory, searchable and fixed format	References to the hard copy document volumes being loaned, or tape/disc numbers used to effect the transfer of soft files (if not across a LAN or WAN), and the number of volumes of such tapes/discs	Configuration control
Comments	Optional and free format	'None' or any comments necessary, e.g. 'Document already on loan', 'Files corrupted—recopy', etc.	Configuration control
Loan/Access confirmation	Mandatory, (unless CIWF cancelled) and fixed format	The name and signature (ink or electronic) of the configuration controller who effected the loan of or access to the CI, together with the date the CI was made available in soft copy, or handed over in hard copy	Configuration control
CIWF closure	Mandatory, validated, searchable and fixed format	Dated signature (ink or electronic) proving that the 'Closure Mini Audit' has been satisfactory (e.g. a document has been returned to the Library)	Configuration manager

APPENDIX A.4 NAMING CONVENTIONS

A.4.1 DOCUMENTATION NAMING CONVENTIONS

Document CI mnemonics should ensure uniqueness throughout a company by being created from, for example, a level (work breakdown structure—WBS), category, type and serial number, as shown in the document naming convention matrix in Figure A4.1.

It is important to remember that the issue number of a document is not part of its identifying mnemonic but is *associated* with it because, otherwise, every time a document is updated, its identifier would change. For example, when the project AAA Quality Plan is updated, its CI identifier will remain AAA-0-0-3-01, with 'Issue 1.00' or 'Issue 2.00' being associated with it as part of its overall status. Some document filing systems, however, make the issue number part of the identifier so that in the case above, the Quality Plan would *change* its identifier from AAA-0-0-3-01-01 to AAA-0-0-3-01-02 which would be incorrect, in configuration management terms, as it would mean that a new CI had been created, not that an existing one had been updated!

A.4.2 SOFTWARE NAMING CONVENTIONS

Unlike documents, software CI names need not be unique at the CI node level, only within the CI path (unless dictated by a CM tool). For example, there might be two projects, each with a 'Detailed Design Document for Office Automation' and each with modules in their software named 'mail'; as the documents are likely to be used in hardcopy and could, therefore, easily become muddled up, they must each have a unique identifying mnemonic, as explained in the previous section. The software, however, is only likely to be accessed in soft copy and so the structure within which it is stored will provide the required uniqueness. To safeguard against a print-out of the 'mail' source code not being unique, the respective directory path should be included in the file header.

Software naming conventions, therefore, can be far less strict than for documents, and be confined to establishing the maximum length (e.g. 6 characters for components and 14 characters for modules) and ensuring that each name is meaningful. These two rules, although simple, are essential so that there is global uniformity. The overall length needs to be kept as short as possible so that there are a minimum amount of keystrokes, so that structure paths are kept as short as possible, and so that as much information as possible may be displayed on a screen without having to scroll. Examples of sensible software names are, therefore:

> OA/mail/send
> OA/mail/receive
> OA/mail/delete
> OA/mail/archive

Description	Project	Level	Category	Type	Serial Number
Project AAA contract	AAA	0	1	0	01
Project AAA system requirements specification	AAA	1	2	1	01
Project AAA hardware specification	AAA	1	3	1	02
Project AAA system interface specification	AAA	1	3	1	03
Project AAA system test plan	AAA	1	4	3	01
Project AAA system test procedure	AAA	1	4	4	01
Project AAA system acceptance test report	AAA	1	4	5	01
Project AAA component test procedure standard	AAA	2	4	2	01
Project AAA component 1 software requirements specification	AAA	2	2	1	01
Project AAA component 1 data definition specification	AAA	2	2	1	02
Project BBB component 1 design specification	BBB	2	3	1	01
Project BBB module B detailed design specification	BBB	3	3	1	01
Project AAA quality plan	AAA	0	0	3	01
Project BBB configuration management plan	BBB	0	0	3	02
Project AAA incident/defect reporting procedure	AAA	0	0	4	02

Key:

LEVEL/WBS	CATEGORY	TYPE
0 = Project/company	0 = Quality	0 = Contract/SLA
1 = System	1 = Commercial	1 = Specification
2 = Component	2 = Requirement	2 = Standard
3 = Module	3 = Design	3 = Plan
	4 = Test	4 = Procedure
	5 = User	5 = Report
	6 = Security	6 = Form
		7 = Manual/guide

Figure A4.1   Example document naming convention matrix

Many operating systems and/or tools will dictate the maximum file name length and/or extension string. Where this is not fixed, and/or where there is a diversity of operating systems, tools and programming languages, it is essential that guidelines, if not rigid conventions, be established early in the project, that these are communicated to all and are then checked for in code reviews.

For example:

- personalized files ('john.test') may be useful for informal use, but must never be allowed to form part of a CI;
- the first principle of version control must be mandated, i.e. that when a file is updated, the name of the file must not change, only its associated version; and
- in a well structured configuration hierarchy, the path will ensure uniqueness to files, so that many characters may be saved in the file name.

A.4.3 BASELINE, RELEASE AND ISSUE NAMING CONVENTIONS

Most projects will include a document version numbering convention in their documentation production standard. Although delivered system version numbers are also usually planned, however, few projects do the same for their *development software*, which is a serious oversight.

A sensible convention for identifying CI status was illustrated in Figure 7.3, i.e. for issue increments to follow the system whereby drafts are always identified by including alphas, and formal issues are identified by being numeric only, for example:

'Issue 1.00A' would be the very first attempt at drafting a new document. As the draft was amended, the issue numbers would change to 'Issue 1.00B', then 'Issue 1.00C', etc., until finally the document was approved at formal review and the alphas would be dropped, so that the document was at 'Issue 1.00'. Further amendment would then produce an 'Issue 2.00A', etc.

The same convention can be used for individual versions of software (and drawings and hardware inventories) as illustrated in Figure 7.3, so that it is clear to all project staff whether they are using a version 'at risk' (i.e. it has an alpha issue status) or one that is under formal configuration control (i.e. numeric issue status).

The use of the alphas to indicate untested software also means that the version numbers do not become too large. The fact that the developer has gone through many iterations to perfect the code should be transparent to everyone but the respective team leader and, possibly, an audit authority.

Once hierarchies of software are being integrated to produce system builds, or documents are being delivered as a complete document set, it can be helpful to introduce more flexible baseline naming conventions. Chapter 9 introduced the concept of 'freezing' sets of CIs together as being common to a particular baseline and these baselines are more easily recognizable if their names are descriptive, rather than purely numeric. Thus baseline naming conventions may dictate a combination of project phase or function (e.g. 'Phase_1', 'OA_2', 'Integ_4'), coupled with the inevitable numeric (and alpha) incrementation to show how many attempts have been made to achieve the fully tested/reviewed product (e.g. 'Phase_1.01', 'OA_2.03', 'Integ_4.01').

The above may seem obvious and simplistic but, where such conventions are not clearly laid down and enforced much confusion can arise, particularly where more than one person needs to access a CI, as can be seen from the following unacceptable but typical set of uncontrolled software release names:

'First', 'Adds Msg.c', 'Temp', '2nd go', 'John's', etc.!

A.4.4 STRUCTURE NODE NAMING CONVENTIONS

In any configuration hierarchy there will be three types of node as illustrated, but not expanded, in Chapter 8. These node types are CIs, 'Sub–CIs' and 'Hooks'. The first, CIs, is obvious and has been concentrated on above (e.g. Project AAA's System Requirements Specification AAA-1-2-1-01). The second, Sub–CIs, simply refers to any node below, or contained in, a CI (e.g. Front, Chapter_1, Chapter_2, etc.). The third, Hooks, are not CIs or parts of CIs, but are useful pegs for hanging CIs on (e.g. requirement documents, test documents, contracts, etc.).

The naming conventions for the first two types, CIs and Sub–CIs, have been dealt with above, since they are documents, inventories, software components, modules or files. It is equally important that all project personnel understand what the Hook nodes will be called, what they will contain underneath them and where in the system configuration they will appear. This, as the future tense implies, must be planned and set up very early in the project life cycle or, if a CM system is being introduced part-way through a project, then early in its introduction.

The system specification tree (SST) illustrated in Figure 8.9 gives examples of all the above naming conventions and, although the conventions will obviously differ for every company and/or project, Figure 8.9 should be a useful template to work from.

A.4.5   CONTROL FORM NUMBERING CONVENTIONS

It should be sufficient for control forms (IDRs, CRs, etc.) simply to be allocated unique, sequential numbers. In some projects/companies, however, it may be helpful to introduce numbering conventions which indicate a category of, say, change request. For example, CRs with numbers 1 to 999 might be reserved for customer changes, while internal CRs would have numbers in the 1000 range.

Another (albeit not strongly recommended) example of where categorization might be used is if a CM system were company-wide and covered several inherited projects; in this case alpha characters might be used as a prefix to a CR number to show which project is impacted. Thus a single report on all open CRs for the entire company might list numbers such as 'FFF-035', 'FFF-036', 'DDD-1134', 'AAA-1235', etc. An extra prefix would have to be reserved, however, for CRs that impact more than one project or the organization itself.

Where there are sub-contractors, another convention is to include their CR number as a suffix so that, for example, a CR raised by the prime contractor which impacts the customer's contract, but which is necessitated because of a suggested change from sub-contractor N, might be numbered '029-N34'.

APPENDIX A.5   MASTER CONFIGURATION INDEX

Figure A5.1 is an example excerpt from a project's master configuration index (MCI),
documenting the latest formal issue of each CI and any impending updates/upgrades.

PROJECT AAA AS AT: 17/02/95	MASTER CONFIGURATION INDEX (MCI)			SORTED ON: CI PATH/ID	
CI_PATH/ID **CI_TITLE**	**CI_OWNER**	**TYPE** **CISF**	**FORMAL** **CI_ISSUE** **CI_STATUS**	**DRAFT** **CI_ISSUE** **CI_STATUS**	
Propsw/700 Sys 700 Patches	Bureau	S/W 336	UX9.01 Released		
Propsw/800 Sys 800 Patches	Bureau	S/W 337	UX9.00 Released		
RTSsw/OA Office Automation Component	F. Petry	S/W 355	Build_3.01 Released	Build_4.00b Testing	
docn/system/req_docs/1-2-1-01 System Requirements Spec	A. Richie	Doc 125	Issue_2.01 Released	Issue_2.02a Await_Files	
docn/system/test_docs/1-4-4-01 System Test Procedure	N. Smith	Doc 201	Issue_2.00 Released		
source/OA/mail mail Module	J. Fagan	S/W 403	OA_3.00 Released		
stnds/dev/2-4-2-01 Component Test Procedure Stnd	F. Allen	Doc 124	Issue_1.00 Released	Issue_1.01c For_Review	
stnds/qa/0-0-3-01 Project Quality Plan	R. Hicks	Doc 209	Issue_2.00 Released		
test/OA Office Automation Test Data	F. Petry	S/W 356	Build_3.01 Released		

Figure A5.1   Excerpt from a master configuration index

APPENDIX A.6 BASELINE REGISTER

Figure A6.1 is an example excerpt from a project's baseline register, illustrating how internal and delivery baselines can be planned and controlled by allocating respective baseline names to each issue/release of each CI.

PROJECT AAA AS AT: 17/02/95	BASELINE REGISTER		SORTED ON: BASELINE
CI__PATH/ID **CI__TITLE**	**CI__TYPE** **CISF__No**	**CI__ISSUE** **CI__STATUS**	**BASELINE**
source/OA/mail Mail Module	S/W 403	OA__3.00 Released	HCI__1
docn/system/req__docs/1-2-1-01 System Requirements Spec	Doc 125	Issue__2.01 Released	Phase__3
Propsw/700 Sys 700 Patches	S/W 336	UX9.01 Released	Sys__Del__1
Propsw/800 Sys 800 Patches	S/W 337	UX9.00 Released	Sys__Del__1
docn/system/req__docs/1-2-1-01 System Requirements Spec	Doc 125	Issue__2.02a Await__Files	Sys__Del__1
docn/system/test__docs/1-4-4-01 System Test Procedure	Doc 201	Issue__2.00 Released	Sys__Del__1
stnds/dev/2-4-2-01 Component Test Procedure Stnd	Doc 124	Issue__1.00 Released	Sys__Del__1
stnds/dev/2-4-2-01 Component Test Procedure Stnd	Doc 124	Issue__1.01c For__Review	Sys__Del__1
stnds/qa/0-0-3-01 Project Quality Plan	Doc 209	Issue__2.00 Released	Sys__Del__1
RTSsw/OA Office Automation Component	S/W 355	Build__3.01 Released	Trial__2
RTSsw/OA Office Automation Component	S/W 355	Build__4.00b Testing	Trial__2
test/OA Office Automation Test Data	S/W 356	Build__3.01 Released	Trial__2

Figure A6.1   Excerpt from a baseline register

APPENDIX A.7   INCIDENT/DEFECT REPORT BASELINE REGISTER

Figure A7.1 is an example excerpt of a project's incident/defect report (IDR) baseline register, illustrating which IDRs will need to be cleared and tested for, to achieve specific baselines.

PROJECT AAA AS AT: 17/02/95		IDR BASELINE REGISTER		SORTED ON: BASELINE
IDR NO	**CI__PATH/ID CI__NAME IDR__TITLE**	**ISSUE__IMPACTED CR (if any)**	**ACTIONEE IDR__STATUS**	**CLEARANCE BASELINE**
236	docn/OA/des__docs/2-3-1-01 OA S/W Design Spec Mail Receive Failure	Issue__1.00 CR__835	R. Allen Awaiting__CR	HCI__1
248	source/OA/mail Mail Module Receive Mail Test Failed	Build__1.01 CR__838	H. Ashton Awaiting__CR	HCI__1
198	source/SYS/login System Login Module Password can be 'hacked'	Integ__3.00	H. Fraser External__Actn	Phase__3
243	stnds/CM/0-0-3-02 Config Management Plan Customer Impact Not Clear	Issue__2.01	M. Wiley For__Sentence	Phase__3
244	stnds/CM/0-0-4-03 Change Control Procedures Add "Customer Impact ?" Box	Issue__2.00	R. Allen Initial__Inv	Phase__3
245	RTSsw Run Time Sytem Software Core Dump if System >85%	Trial__1.02	Maj Frenny Detailed__Inv	Trial__2

Figure A7.1   Excerpt from an incident/defect report baseline register

APPENDIX A.8   CHANGE REQUEST (CR) BASELINE REGISTER

Figure A8.1 is an example excerpt of a project's change request (CR) baseline register, illustrating which change requests will need to be implemented to achieve specific baselines.

PROJECT AAA AS AT: 17/02/95	CR BASELINE REGISTER		SORTED ON: BASELINE
CR NO	CI_PATH/ID CI_NAME CR_TITLE	ISSUE_IMPACTED NEW_ISSUE	ACTIONEE CR_STATUS	CLEARANCE BASELINE
805	docn/system/req_docs/1-2-1-01/vol II Req Spec Vol II Change to Mail HCI	Issue_1.01 Issue_2.00	Config Ctrl Approved	HCI_1
834	docn/OA/req_docs/2-2-1-01 OA S/W Req Spec Additional Mail Option	Issue_1.00 Issue_2.00	R. Allen Approved	HCI_1
835	docn/OA/des_docs/2-3-1-01 OA S/W Design Spec Change to Mail Menu	Issue_1.00 Issue_2.00	R. Allen Approved	HCI_1
838	source/OA/mail Mail Module Addition of Mail Archive	Build_1.03 Build_1.04	H. Ashton For_Review	HCI_1
775	docn/system/req_docs/1-2-1-01/vol I Req Spec Vol I Password Encryption	Issue_1.00 Issue_1.01	Tech Docs Implementing	Phase_3
781	docn/system/req_docs/1-2-1-01/vol I Req Spec Vol I Plotter Specification	Issue_1.00 Issue_1.01	Tech Docs Implementing	Phase_3
785	docn/system/req_docs/1-2-1-01/vol III Req Spec Vol III Change to Screen Sizes	Issue_2.00 Issue_2.01	S. Timpson For_Review	Phase_4

Figure A8.1   Excerpt from a change request baseline register

APPENDIX A.9 INCIDENT/DEFECT REPORT (IDR) FIELDS

Table A9.1   Incident/defect report (IDR) fields

Field name	Attributes	Description	Completed/amended by
IDR security classification	Mandatory (in classified projects), validated, searchable and fixed format	Entries such as 'Unclassified', 'Restricted', 'Commercial-in-confidence', etc.	Originator and TRC chairman
Sheet n of n	Mandatory and fixed format	Not only the respective sheet number, but also the total number of sheets including all attachments, so that none may be lost in hardcopy format	Originator and investigators
IDR no	Mandatory, validated, searchable and fixed format	A unique, sequential number preferably allocated by a CM tool, but could be from a log book	Configuration control (or CM tool)
IDR title	Mandatory, searchable and fixed format	A short string which uniquely identifies the IDR contents	Originator
Urgency	Mandatory, validated, searchable and fixed format	One of 'Very Urgent', 'Urgent', 'Normal' or 'Long Term' to indicate how quickly the IDR needs to be investigated and cleared. An alternative to this field is a 'Severity Rating'	Originator, investigators and TRC chairman
Associated forms	Optional, searchable and fixed format	Reference to any other IDRs or change requests that may impact the same subject or CI	Originator, investigators and TRC chairman
External reference(s)	Optional, searchable and fixed format	Reference to any relevant sub-contractor and/or customer configuration control or help desk forms	Originator and investigators
IDR status	Mandatory, validated, searchable and fixed format	Dependent on the exact procedure being followed, will contain options such as 'Draft', 'Initial Investigation', 'Detailed Investigation', 'Cancelled', 'Cleared', 'External Action', etc., to describe what is happening to the IDR	Configuration control
Actionee	Mandatory, searchable and fixed format	The name (or user account for electronic CM systems) of the person currently carrying out the actions described in the Status field. (Note: for 'External Action', the sub-contractor company must also be entered)	Configuration control

Table A9.1 (continued)

Field name	Attributes	Description	Completed/ amended by
Status date	Mandatory, validated, searchable and fixed format	The date on which the status changed (or the IDR was raised if status = 'Draft')	Configuration control
Action due date	Mandatory, validated, searchable and fixed format	The date by which the action described in the status field must be completed by the actionee and the IDR returned (or mailed) to CM or to the next actionee	Configuration control
CI project	Mandatory, validated, searchable and fixed format	The name of the project on which the incident or defect has occurred. (If only one project is being controlled, then the project name should be set by an automatic default)	Originator
CI ID and title	Mandatory, validated, searchable and fixed format	The defective CI's unique identifier e.g. '1-3-1-01' and title e.g. 'System Architecture Design' and its exact path in the SST. (Note: this may not be known when the form is first raised and so should be added in)	Originator or investigators
CI issue/ release number	Mandatory, validated, searchable and fixed format	The unique issue status of the defective CI, e.g. 'Issue 2.01'. (Note: may not be known at first and so should be added in)	Originator or investigators
Description of incident or defect	Mandatory and free text	Full description of what the user was doing and what went wrong or seemed to be incorrect	Originator
Interim action	Optional and free text	Full description of any action taken when the incident occurred or the defect was discovered, e.g. the names of files patched (and how) or the mark-ups entered into a document	Originator
Originator details	Mandatory, searchable and fixed format	The name and dated signature (ink or electronic) of the person reporting the incident or defect. (Note: where the IDR procedure spans more than one company, e.g. to include the customer or sub-contractor(s), the originator's organization name must also be included)	Originator
Distribution	Optional and fixed format	List of project personnel, if any, who should be made aware of the IDR even before it is investigated	Originator or configuration control
Keywords	Optional, searchable and fixed format	Two or three subjects with which the IDR could be associated or identified, e.g. 'Clause 5', 'Formal Test', 'Comms', etc.	Originator and investigators

Table A9.1   (continued)

Field name	Attributes	Description	Completed/amended by
Initial investigation assignee	Mandatory and fixed format	The name of the person who is the 'Owner' of the defective CI (i.e. responsible for its development or maintenance)	Configuration control
Initial investigation report	Mandatory and free text	Initial investigator's findings and recommendations	Initial investigator
Detailed investigation assignee	Optional and fixed format	The name of the person requested to investigate the IDR further, if the initial investigation has been inconclusive	TRC chairman
Detailed investigation report	Optional and free text	Detailed investigator's findings and recommendations	Detailed investigator
Sentence	Mandatory, validated, searchable and fixed format	Dependent on the exact procedures being followed, will contain options such as 'Cancel', 'Raise CR', 'Create CI', 'Concede', etc.	TRC chairman
Clearance baseline	Mandatory, (unless IDR cancelled) validated, searchable and fixed format	The name of the baseline by which the IDR is to be cleared (or conceded) e.g. the name of the software build in which the defect will be tested for clearance	TRC chairman
Clearance assignee	Mandatory, (unless IDR cancelled) searchable and fixed format	The name of the person responsible for clearing the IDR (usually the defective CI's 'Owner'), or QA if the IDR has been conceded	TRC chairman
Clearance refs	Mandatory, (unless IDR cancelled) validated, searchable and fixed format	The type and number of the form that clears or concedes the IDR, e.g. 'Concession 9', 'CR 238', 'CISF 89', etc.	Clearance assignee
IDR closure	Mandatory, validated, searchable and fixed format	Dated signature (ink or electronic) proving that the 'Closure Mini Audit' has been satisfactory	Configuration manager

APPENDIX A.10   CHANGE REQUEST (CR) FIELDS

Table A10.1   Change request (CR) fields

Field name	Attributes	Description	Completed/ amended by
CR security classification	Mandatory (in classified projects), validated, searchable and fixed format	Entries such as 'Unclassified', 'Restricted', 'Commercial-in-Confidence', etc.	Originator, reviewers and TRC chairman
Sheet n of n	Mandatory and fixed format	Not only the respective sheet number, but also the total number of sheets including all attachments, so that none may be lost in hardcopy format	Originator
CR no	Mandatory, validated, searchable and fixed format	A unique, sequential number preferably allocated by a CM tool, but could be from a log book	Configuration control (or CM tool)
CR title	Mandatory, searchable and fixed format	A short string which uniquely identifies the CR contents and describes the change subject	Originator
Change priority	Mandatory, validated, searchable and fixed format	One of 'Immediate', 'High', 'Medium' or 'Low' to indicate how quickly the CR needs to be reviewed and implemented	Originator, reviewers and TRC chairman
Change purpose	Mandatory, validated, searchable and fixed format	One of 'Enhancement' or 'Repair'	Originator, reviewers and TRC chairman
Change type	Mandatory, validated, searchable and fixed format	One of 'External' or 'Internal' to indicate whether or not the change would impact the customer/user	Originator
Associated forms	Optional, searchable and fixed format	Reference to any other IDRs or change requests that may impact the same subject or CI	Originator, reviewers and TRC chairman
CR source	Mandatory, searchable and free text	Reference to another CR or IDR, meeting minutes or correspondence which has necessitated the proposed change to the CI	Originator
CR status	Mandatory, validated, searchable and fixed format	Dependent on the exact procedure being followed, will contain options such as 'Draft', 'For Recommendation', 'For Review/Assessment', 'For Rework', 'For Approval', 'Cancelled', 'Implementing', 'Closed', etc., to describe what is happening to the CR	Configuration control

Table A10.1 (continued)

Field name	Attributes	Description	Completed/ amended by
Actionee	Mandatory, searchable and fixed format	The name (or user account for electronic CM systems) of the person currently carrying out the actions described in the status field	Configuration control
Status date	Mandatory, validated, searchable and fixed format	The date on which the status changed (or the CR was raised if status = 'Draft')	Configuration control
Action due date	Mandatory, validated, searchable and fixed format	The date by which the action described in the status field must be completed by the actionee and the CR returned (or mailed back) to CM	Configuration control
Progression rating	Mandatory, validated, searchable and fixed format	One of 0 to 6, as calculated from the priority, category and type fields (see Chapter 13)	Configuration control
CI project	Mandatory, validated, searchable and fixed format	The name of the project of which the CI to be changed is part. (If only one project is being controlled, then the project name should be set by an automatic default)	Originator
CI ID and title	Mandatory, validated, searchable and fixed format	The changing CI's unique identifier e.g. '1-3-1-01' and title e.g. 'System Architecture Design' and its exact path in the SST	Originator
CI issue/release number	Mandatory, validated, searchable and fixed format	The unique issue status of the CI to be changed, e.g. 'Issue 2.01'	Originator
CR category	Mandatory, validated, searchable and fixed format	One of 'Minor', 'Moderate' or 'Major' to indicate whether the proposed change will need to be reviewed by the originator's own group only, project wide or by the customer	Originator, reviewers and TRC chairman
Distribution	Mandatory and fixed format	List of project personnel who should review the proposed change(s), assess the impact, suggest a clearance baseline, etc.	Originator, configuration control and TRC chairman
Keywords	Mandatory, validated, searchable and fixed format	Two or three subjects with which the CR could be associated or identified, e.g. 'Clause 5', 'Formal Test', 'Comms', etc.	Originator, reviewers and TRC chairman

Table A10.1 (continued)

Field name	Attributes	Description	Completed/ amended by
Proposed change	Mandatory and free text	Description of why and how the CI would be changed, if recommended for progression (excluding the required mark-ups to the document CI or changed software CI listings—i.e. tasks or resources/time estimates—at this stage)	Originator
Originator details	Mandatory, searchable and fixed format	The name and dated signature (ink or electronic) of the person proposing the change (Note: where the CR procedure spans more than one company, e.g. to include the customer or sub-contractor(s), the originator's organization name must also be included)	Originator
Recommender details	Mandatory, searchable and fixed format	The name and dated signature (ink or electronic) of the person recommending that the originator fully investigate the change and mark-up the document CI or change the development version of the software CI, etc., as applicable, for progression of the CR	Recommender (who is also the first reviewer, if the CR is recommended)
Impact analysis (assessment)	Mandatory, searchable and fixed format	A list of other CIs or CI types, e.g. 'Software Design Docs', which could be impacted by the proposed change or references to either other resulting CRs or tasks sheets. Estimated time, resources and cost gain/loss should also be included. The fields must be initialled by the reviewers carrying out the assessment	Originator, line manager, reviewers and TRC chairman
Review comments	Mandatory and free text	Initialled and dated comments (ink or electronic) by reviewers on the details of the change, e.g. 'OK', 'Para 2.4.3 should be reworded', 'Don't understand sctn 3', 'Will this necessitate parallel development?' etc.	Reviewers
Comments response	Mandatory and free text	Initialled and dated response to each review comment, e.g. 'DFJ's comment valid—sheet 8 reworked', 'Suggest meeting to discuss comment 9', etc.	Originator

Table A10.1 (continued)

Field name	Attributes	Description	Completed/ amended by
TRC approval	Mandatory, validated, searchable and fixed format	Dependent on the exact procedures being followed, will contain options such as 'Approved', 'Rejected', 'Conceded', etc., signed and dated (ink or electronic) by the TRC chairman	TRC chairman
Customer CR cross-ref	Mandatory, validated, searchable and fixed format	Either 'n/a' or a customer change request number that has resulted from the approval of the internal CR	Configuration control
Clearance baseline	Mandatory, (unless CR cancelled) validated, searchable and fixed format	The name of the baseline by which the CR is to be implemented (or conceded) e.g. the name of the software build in which the change will be tested	TRC chairman
Implementation instructions	Optional and free text	Information such as 'This CR must be implemented after CR 236'	TRC chairman
Implementor	Mandatory (unless CR cancelled), searchable and fixed format	The name of the person responsible for implementing the changes proposed in the CR, if approved, i.e. the changing CI's 'Owner', or QA if the CR has been conceded	Configuration control
Clearance refs	Mandatory (unless CR cancelled), searchable and fixed format	The type and number of the form/ report that documents successful implementation of the changes or concedes the CR, e.g. 'CISF 189' or 'Concession 7'. To be signed and dated (ink or electronic) by the clearance assignee	Clearance assignee
Task actuals	Mandatory, searchable and fixed format	Actual times, resources and cost gain/ loss, compared to those estimated during impact analysis	Implementor and line manager
CR closure	Mandatory, validated, searchable and fixed format	Dated signature (ink or electronic) proving that the 'Closure Mini Audit' has been satisfactory	Configuration manager

APPENDIX A.11   CM AUDIT CHECK LIST

1. Organization and responsibilities

    1.1 Management structure

    1.2 Interface to other projects

    1.3 Interface to customer

    1.4 Interface to sub-contractor(s)

2. CM documentation

    2.1 Policies/plans

    2.2 Procedures

    2.3 Work instructions

    2.4 Manuals/user guides

    2.5 Configuration control forms

3. Configuration identification

4. Configuration control

    4.1 Submissions

    4.2 The controlled area/library

    4.3 Baselines

    4.4 Distribution

    4.5 Defect/non-conformance reporting

    4.6 Change control

5. Status accounting

    5.1 Master Configuration index (MCI)

    5.2 System specification tree (SST)

    5.3 Control form registers/reports

    5.4 Build state logs

6. Configuration auditing

7. System integrity

    7.1 The development and target environments

    7.2 System failure

    7.3 Backing up

    7.4 Archiving/off-lining

1. ORGANIZATION AND RESPONSIBILITIES

1.1 Management structure

1.1.1 Are the responsibilities and incumbents of the following roles (or their equivalents) documented, relative to CM?

(a) Project manager
(b) Configuration manager
(c) Quality assurance manager/representative
(d) Technical authority
(e) Group/team leaders
(f) TRC/CCB/CCRB chairmen and members
(g) Project configuration controller(s)

1.2 Interface to other projects

1.2.1 Does the CM system cover more than one project and, if so, are the respective project CIs clearly segregated and controlled in terms of access?

1.2.2 Is authorization required in order to pass CIs between projects and, if so, is this proceduralized?

1.3 Interface to customer

1.3.1 Does the documentation detail who shall be the point of contact for matters relating to CM within both the contractor's and customer's organizations?

1.3.2 Are the actions necessary for opening, progressing and closing configuration control forms to and from the customer clearly defined?

1.3.3 Are the authorized customer signatories for incident/defect reports and change requests clearly defined?

1.3.4 Are customer delivery baselines clearly defined in terms of reference (names) and timescale (dates)?

1.3.5 Do the procedures ensure that actions placed at customer meetings will be monitored?

1.4 Interface to sub-contractor(s)

1.4.1 Does the documentation detail who shall be the point of contact for matters relating to CM within both the contractor's and sub-contractor's organizations?

1.4.2 Are the actions necessary for opening, progressing and closing configuration control forms to and from the sub-contractor(s) clearly defined?

1.4.3   Are the authorized sub-contractor signatories for incident/defect reports and change requests clearly defined?

1.4.4   Are sub-contractor delivery baselines clearly defined in terms of reference (names) and timescale (dates)?

2.   CM DOCUMENTATION

2.1   *Policies/plans*

2.1.1   Is there a document such as a CM plan outlining the policies to be followed for CM on the project?

2.1.2   Do CM personnel have access to the project contract (or other relevant document or plan) which gives details of the project's development, warranty and maintenance timescales?

2.2   *Procedures*

2.2.1   Are the CM procedures clearly documented?

2.2.2   Are the procedures comprehensive, i.e. do they cover all the disciplines of CM (configuration identification, configuration control, status accounting and configuration auditing)?

2.2.3   Are the procedures linked to their higher-level policy document?

2.2.4   Do the procedures reference the respective company/project quality documentation?

2.3   *Work instructions*

2.3.1   Do work instructions, giving details of exactly how to run the CM system, exist (either as stand-alone document(s) or as part of the procedures) and, if so, are they accessible to all configuration controllers?

2.4   *Manuals/user guides*

2.4.1   Do manuals and/or user guides exist for the CM tool(s) and the operating system/environment on which it resides and are they accessible to all configuration controllers?

2.5   *Configuration control forms*

2.5.1   Are master and/or blank/softcopy forms accessible to all controllers and project personnel and, if so, is that access controlled?

2.5.2   Are different versions of forms identified so that it is clear which is the current, valid version of any form?

2.5.3 Do the procedures illustrate the forms and detail how they should be used?

3. CONFIGURATION IDENTIFICATION

3.1 Is there a CI plan or equivalent document?

3.2 Are CIs and their issue status uniquely identified?

3.3 Are the relationships of CIs and groups of CIs clearly defined and documented?

3.4 Can software/hardware CIs be traced to the document CIs that defined them?

3.5 Do document CIs clearly reference the software/ hardware CIs they define?

3.6 Are CI types (i.e. development/draft or issue) unambiguously identified?

3.7 Are requisite naming conventions for CIs, issues and baselines detailed in the CM procedures or other project documentation?

4. CONFIGURATION CONTROL

4.1 *Submissions*

4.1.1 Is there evidence that software CIs have been successfully dry run tested prior to submission to the CM controlled area?

4.1.2 Is there evidence that document/inventory CIs have been successfully reviewed prior to submission to the CM controlled area?

4.1.3 Is there a mechanism for documenting and following up on any known deficiencies in a CI at the time of submission?

4.1.4 Are source code CIs clearly linked to their resulting executables?

4.1.5 Are executables clearly linked back to the originating source CIs?

4.1.6 Are test specifications/plans and procedures controlled, together with their resulting test reports/logs?

4.1.7 Are test programs and data controlled and linked to the software/hardware they test?

4.1.8 If a CI is being re-submitted, is the change documentation traceable?

4.2 *The controlled area/library*

4.2.1 Is there a dedicated CM processor or partition of a processor (i.e. a controlled area and electronic library)?

4.2.2 Is read/copy/use access to the controlled area planned and controlled?

4.2.3 Is update access to the controlled area restricted to CM personnel?

4.2.4 Is there a locked room/cabinet for hardcopy document and inventory CIs (i.e. a document library)?

4.2.5 Are hardcopy masters of all document and inventory CIs kept in the document library?

4.2.6 Are lending copies of document and inventory CIs kept in the document library?

4.2.7 Is it possible to list all document and/or inventory CIs on loan, in terms of when they were borrowed/returned and by whom?

4.3 Baselines

4.3.1 Is it possible to list all the CIs and their respective issues that comprise a given baseline?

4.3.2 Is it possible to list all control forms and their status that affect the CIs of any given baseline?

4.3.3 Is it possible to repeat a build of a baseline CI (i.e. withdraw the same CIs at their same versions and use the same version of the compiler on the same version of the operating system, etc.) and to prove that it is the same?

4.4 Distribution

4.4.1 Are CIs always submitted to the controlled area prior to being distributed?

4.4.2 Is there a procedure for ensuring that only the latest issue of a document or inventory CI is available for loan, unless a previous issue is specifically requested?

4.4.3 Is there a procedure for ensuring that only the latest issue of a software CI or software baseline is available for use, unless an earlier one is specifically required?

4.4.4 Can it be proven that CIs tested during a dry run test are identical to those used in the ensuing formal test?

4.4.5 Are tapes/discs used for distributing/receiving CI files clearly identified with the CI ID, title and issue?

4.4.6 Can the whereabouts of all tapes/discs containing CIs be traced?

4.4.7 Can the whereabouts of all hardware CIs be traced?

4.5 Defect/non-conformance reporting

4.5.1 Can CIs that may be affected by a reported defect or non-conformance be identified?

4.5.2 Is there a procedure for ensuring that users of CIs that may be defective are informed of the details in defect report(s), or equivalent form(s)?

4.5.3 Are defect reports uniquely identified?

4.5.4 Are defect reports linked to the respective change request(s) (or equivalent form) that clears them?

4.5.5 Can all reported defects on any one CI be listed and the details accessed?

4.5.6 Is the status and whereabouts (i.e. paper location or electronic life-cycle stage) of a defect report known and demonstrable at all times?

4.5.7 Does the defect report document which level of the CI structure may be defective (e.g. system/sub-system/component/module/file)?

4.5.8 Does the defect report document any interim action that may have been taken (e.g. a software 'patch' installed)?

4.5.9 Is there effective recording and control for defect reports that have been investigated and sentenced, but which are not to be closed until some future specified condition is met (e.g. successful dry run testing of the defective CI)?

4.5.10 Is there a procedure for ensuring that defective hardware CIs are segregated from the operative/live system?

4.6 Change control

4.6.1 Are CIs that may be affected by a proposed change identified on change requests?

4.6.2 Is there a procedure for ensuring that the original reviewers (or their equivalents) of a CI that may be changing are informed of the details of the proposed change and given the opportunity to re-review?

4.6.3 Are change requests uniquely identified?

4.6.4 Is the source/origin of a change request documented (e.g. an incident/defect report, meeting minutes, formal test)?

4.6.5 Can all proposed, cancelled and/or implemented change requests on any one CI be listed and the details accessed?

4.6.6   Is the status and whereabouts (i.e. paper location or electronic life-cycle stage) of a change request known and demonstrable at all times?

4.6.7   Are change requests linked to the respective CI submission forms (or similar implementation records) that clear them, i.e. is there a procedure for ensuring that authorized changes/modifications are implemented?

4.6.8   Do change requests document whether or not the proposed change impacts the customer and/or sub-contractor(s)?

4.6.9   Do change requests document whether the proposed change is to repair, modify or both?

4.6.10 Do change requests indicate *estimated* resources, timescales and costs for implementation and are the *actual* resources, timescales and costs recorded and compared?

4.6.11 Do change requests give full details of the proposed change, such that interested parties and future maintainers will understand exactly what the change is and why it has been proposed?

4.6.12 Is there effective recording and control for changes that have been authorized but which are not to be implemented until some future specified condition is met (e.g. authorization of another change request)?

5.   STATUS ACCOUNTING

5.1   *Master configuration index (MCI)*

5.1.1   Is an MCI, covering all CIs, produced regularly or automatically, and distributed or made available in soft and/or hard format, to all project personnel?

5.1.2   Are all copies of the MCI, whether soft or hard, clearly dated so that their validity is known for specific baselines?

5.1.3   Is there a master copy of the current MCI which is held in another location or fire safe?

5.2   *System specification tree (SST)*

5.2.1   Is an SST produced regularly or automatically, and distributed or made available in soft and/or hard format, to all project personnel?

5.2.2   Are all copies of the SST, whether soft or hard, clearly dated so that their validity is known for specific baselines?

5.2.3   Is there evidence of compatibility between the MCI and SST, and is this checked regularly?

5.3   Control form registers/reports

5.3.1   Are registers/reports for each type of form produced regularly or automatically, and distributed or made available in soft and/or hard format, to all project personnel?

5.3.2   Are all registers/reports clearly dated so that their validity is known for specific baselines?

5.3.3   Is it possible to identify which, if any, CIs have concessions on them and to access the details of such concessions?

5.4   Build state logs

5.4.1   Is there evidence that software and hardware distributions/installations are accompanied by build state logs or similar documentation?

5.4.2   Can the build state log for any baseline CI be repeated?

6.   CONFIGURATION AUDITING

6.1   Is there evidence that CM procedural conformance is audited/monitored on a regular basis, by the configuration manager and by quality assurance?

6.2   Do audit trails exist and are they accessible?

6.3   Is it possible to prove the integrity of the MCI, SST and build state logs?

7.   SYSTEM INTEGRITY

7.1   The development and target environments

7.1.1   Is there an inventory CI for all hardware used on the project for development and/or testing of the deliverable system?

7.1.2   Is there a procedure for planning, controlling and recording upgrades to such hardware?

7.1.3   Is there an inventory CI for all proprietary software used on the project for development and/or testing of the deliverable system (e.g. operating system, compiler, word processor)?

7.1.4   Is there a procedure for planning, controlling and recording upgrades to such proprietary software?

7.1.5   Is the development environment (i.e. the hardware plus proprietary and system configuration software) planned, controlled and recorded for each formal test and delivery baseline?

7.1.6 Is the target environment (i.e. the delivered hardware plus proprietary and system configuration software) planned, controlled and recorded for each delivery baseline and throughout warranty and maintenance?

7.2 *System failure*

7.2.1 Do procedures exists which give details of the actions to be taken in the event of CM processor crash and/or a crash of the CM tool(s)?

7.2.2 Is a log kept of CM processor failures and tool(s) crashes?

7.3 *Backing up*

7.3.1 Do procedures exist for backing up the CM system and do they appear to be adequate?

7.3.2 Are the back-up tapes/discs kept in a fire safe?

7.3.3 Are additional copies of the back-up tapes/discs stored off-site?

7.3.4 Is a log kept of all back-up media?

7.4 *Archiving/off-lining*

7.4.1 Are the actions required to archive and/or restore individual and/or baseline CIs clearly documented?

7.4.2 Is there suitable, safe and secure storage provided for archived document and software CIs, whether in soft or hard copy format?

APPENDIX A.12 TRC, CCB AND CCRB AGENDAS

Examples of agendas that might be used in Technical Review Committee (TRC), Configuration Control Board (CCB) and Customer Configuration Review Board (CCRB) meetings.

TRC AGENDA
- Approval of previous minutes
- Actions arising
- Review/update of IDRs/CRs raised since last meeting
- Review/update of urgent or overdue CISFs/IDRs/CRs
- Flag of customer CRs affecting development/testing
- Build/baseline planning
- A.O.B.

CCB AGENDA
- Approval of previous minutes
- Actions arising
- Internal change requests with customer impact
- Customer change requests for review/recommendation
- Sub-contractor delivery baselines—planned and actual
- Customer delivery baselines—planned and actual
- A.O.B.

CCRB AGENDA
- Approval of previous minutes
- Actions arising
- Customer change requests for review/approval
- Contract/SLA issue status
- System delivery baselines
- A.O.B.

APPENDIX A.14   CI TRANSFER MEDIA FORM (TMF) FIELDS

Table A14.1   CI transfer media form (TMF) fields

Field name	Attributes	Description	Completed/ amended by
Fire safe cross-reference	Mandatory, searchable and fixed format	A cross-reference to the bureau or system support numbering system for controlling transfer media off-site or in a fire safe	Configuration control
TMF no	Mandatory, validated, searchable and fixed format	A unique, sequential number preferably allocated by a CM tool, but could be from a log book. (Note: once allocated, this number remains linked to the disc/tape first associated with it, i.e. if the disc/tape becomes corrupted, the respective TMF status should be 'Destroyed', but the TMF number may not be re-used. Likewise, if new data is copied to a disc/tape, then the respective TMF must be updated with the new information)	Configuration control (or CM tool)
Vol n of n	Mandatory, validated, searchable and fixed format	These fields allow for data from one tape/disc to run over into a number of subsequent tapes/discs; the default should be '1 of 1'	Configuration control
Associated TMFs	Validated, searchable and fixed format	The numbers of any other TMF(s) associated with the CI(s) on this TMF, e.g. a second or third volume. Another example is that one DAT might contain test data for a particular build, while another DAT contained the run-time software to be tested	Configuration control
Medium	Mandatory, validated, searchable and fixed format	Dependent on the development/ maintenance platform, will contain entries such as 'DAT', '5.25 disc', '3.5 disc', etc.	Configuration control
TMF status	Mandatory, validated, searchable and fixed format	Dependent on the exact procedure being followed, will contain options such as 'In Use', 'Available', 'Delivered', 'Corrupted', etc., to describe what is happening to the tape/disc	Configuration control
Status date	Mandatory, validated, searchable and fixed format	The date on which the status of the tape/disc and, thus, the TMF changed	Configuration control

Table A14.1 (continued)

Field name	Attributes	Description	Completed/ amended by
CI project	Mandatory, validated, searchable and fixed format	The name of the project to which the CI(s) on the tape/disc belongs. (If only one project is being controlled, then the project name should be set by an automatic default)	Configuration control
CI ID and title	Mandatory, validated, searchable and fixed format	The unique identifier, e.g. '1-3-5-01' and title, e.g. 'System Architecture Design' of the CI(s) on the tape/disc, and its exact path in the SST	Configuration control
CI issue/release number	Mandatory, validated, searchable and fixed format	The unique, new issue or release status of the CI(s) on the tape/disc, e.g. 'Issue 2.01'	Configuration control
CI baseline	Validated, searchable and fixed format	The name of the baseline to which this particular issue of the CI(s) is linked, e.g. a customer delivery, if applicable	Configuration control
CI classification	Mandatory (in classified projects), validated, searchable and fixed format	The highest security classification of the CI(s) on the tape/disc, e.g. 'Unclassified', 'Restricted', 'Commercial-in-Confidence', etc.	Configuration control
CI owner details	Mandatory, searchable and fixed format	The name of the person who has submitted the CI(s) on the tape/disc to configuration control	Configuration control
Reason for transfer	Mandatory and free text	Entries such as a cross reference to a CISF, CIWF or delivery note, or a text explanation such as 'copy of CM Plan for use by Bid Team'	Configuration control
Medium location	Mandatory, searchable and free text	Entries such as 'Firesafe', 'With F. Bloggs', 'With QA', etc., indicating where the 'Master' and/or 'Working Copy' of the tape/disc is	Configuration control
TMF closure	Validated, searchable and fixed format	Dependent on the exact procedures being used, the TMF may be 'Closed' if the tape/disc is delivered or corrupted, i.e. it will never be available for use/reuse again. In this case, these fields would contain the dated signature (ink or electronic) that confirms that the TMF should be closed	Configuration manager

APPENDIX A.15 TRANSFER MEDIA REGISTER

Figure A15.1 is an example excerpt of a project's transfer media register, showing what versions of what CIs are held on tapes/discs, the locations of the media and any cross-reference information required.

PROJECT AAA AS AT: 17/02/95	TRANSFER MEDIA REGISTER		SORTED ON: TMF NO.	
TMF NO **CI PATH/ID** **ASSOCIATED FORMS** **Ci TITLE**		**MEDIA**	**FIRE-REF** **LOCATION** **CI ISSUE**	**STATUS** **DATE**
135	RTSsw/OA 136 Office Automation Component	DAT	0542 With QA Build__3.01	In-Use 27/11/93
136	test/OA 135 Office Automation Test Data	3.50	0543 With QA Build__3.01	In-Use 27/11/93
137	test/accept/data 138 139 Site 43 Test Data	5.25	0550 On-Site Iss__4.01	Deliv'd 28/11/93
138	test/accept/data 137 139 Site 44 Test Data	5.25	0561 On-Site Iss__2.02	Deliv'd 29/11/93
139	RTSsw/ 137 138 Run Time System	DAT	0563 On-Site Build__2.00	Deliv'd 12/12/93
140	Propsw/700 141 Sys 700 Patches	DAT	0575 Firesafe UX9.01	Stored 27/01/94
141	Propsw/800 140 Sys 800 Patches	DAT	0576 Firesafe UX9.00	Stored 27/01/94

Figure A15.1   Excerpt from a transfer media register

APPENDIX A.16 TOOL FUNCTIONS CHECK LIST

Table A16.1 Tool functions check list

(continued)

Tool	CCC/ Harvest	Clear Case	CM Vision	Continuus	LIFESPAN	PCMS	PVCS	Red Box	SCCS
Developers	Softool Corps Inc., USA	Atria Software Inc., USA	Experware Inc., USA	Continuus Software Corp., USA	BAeSEMA Ltd, UK	SQL Software Ltd, UK	Intersolv, Ltd, UK	Ultracomp Ltd	AT&T
UK suppliers	Softool Ltd	Atria Software Ltd	ISDE Ltd	Continuus Software Ltd	BAeSEMA Ltd	SQL Software Ltd	Systems FX Ltd	Ultracomp Ltd	
FUNCTIONS									
Interfaces									
Graphical user interface	Y	Y	Y	Y	Y	Y	Y	Y	
Menu user interface	Y	Y	Y	Y	Y	Y	Y	N	N
Command line interface	Y	Y	Y	Y	Y	Y	Y	N	Y
Command macro facility	Y	Y	Y	Y	Y	Y	Y	N	N
Application programmer interface	Y	Y	Y	Y	Y	Y	Y	Y	N
Easy/intuitive to use	Y	Y	Y	Y	Y	N	Y	Y	Y
Uncomplex initial set up and load	Y	Y	Y	Y	Y	N	N	Y	Y
CIs and structures									
Source/ASCII text control	Y	Y	Y	Y	Y	Y	Y	N	Y
Executables control	N	Y	Y	Y	Y	Y	N	N	N
Source to execs link	Y	Y	N	Y	Y	Y	N	N	N
File versioning	Y	Y	Y	Y	Y	Y	Y	Y	Y
Build/make support	Y	Y	Y	Y	Y	Y	Y	N	N
File merging	Y	Y	Y	Y	N	Y	N	N	N
Parallel development support	Y	Y	Y	Y	Y	Y	N	N	N
Easy hierarchy duplication	N	Y	Y	Y	Y	N	N	N	N
File and/or CI linking	Y	Y	Y	Y	Y	Y	N	N	N
Hierarchical releases	N	Y	Y	Y	Y	Y	Y	N	N
Tailored release naming	Y	Y	Y	Y	Y	Y	Y	N	N
CI link to config ctrl forms	N	N	Y	Y	Y	Y	N	N	N

CIs and structures (continued) / **Disc space utilization** / **Configuration control forms** / **Integrity** / **Status accounting**

Feature										
CIs and structures (continued)										
Previous release access	Y	Y	Y	Y	Y	Y	Y	Y	Z	Y
Previous file version access	Y	Y	Y	Y	Y	Y	Y	Y	Z	Y
CI lifecycle event triggering	Y	N	Y	Y	Y	Y	N	Y	Z	N
Disc space utilization										
File forward-deltaing	Z	Z	Y	Y	Z	Y	Z	Y	Z	Z
File reverse-deltaing	Z	Z	Y	Y	Z	Y	Z	Y	Z	Z
Proprietary deltaing	Y	Z	Y	Z	Z	Z	Y	Z	Z	Z
Data compression support	Z	Z	Y	Z	Y	Z	Y	Y	Z	Z
Archive/restore facility	Z	Y	Y	Y	Y	Y	Y	Y	Z	Z
File and/or hierarchy delete facility	Y	Y	N	Y	Y	Y	Y	Y	N	Z
Configuration control forms										
Smart forms creation	Z	Z	Y	Y	Y	Y	Z	N	Z	Z
Forms link to CIs	Z	Y	Y	Y	Y	Y	Y	Y	Y	Y
Customizable forms interface	Z	Y	Y	Y	Y	Y	Y	Y	Y	Y
Forms event triggering	Y	Y	Y	Y	Y	Y	Y	Y	Y	Y
Forms fields validation	Z	Y	Y	Y	Z	Y	Y	Y	Z	Z
Forms fields arithmetic	Z	Y	N	Z	Y	Y	Y	Y	Z	Y
Auto unique sequential numbering	Z	Y	Y	Y	Y	Y	Y	Y	Y	Y
Integrity										
File level access control	Z	Y	Y	Y	Y	Y	Y	Y	Y	Y
Hierarchy level access control	Y	Y	Z	Y	Y	Y	Y	Y	Y	Z
Root/'SuperUser' access control	Z	Y	Y	Z	Z	Y	Y	Z	N	Z
User access control	Z	Y	N	Y	Y	Y	Y	Y	Y	Y
Roles access control	Y	Z	Z	Y	Y	Z	Z	Z	Y	Y
Audit trails	Y	Y	Y	Y	Y	Y	Y	Y	Y	Y
Error message reporting	Y	Y	Y	Y	Y	Y	Y	Y	Y	Y
Status accounting										
CI build state reporting	Y	Y	Y	Y	Y	Y	Y	Y	Y	Y
File difference reporting	Y	Y	Y	Y	Y	Y	Y	Y	Y	Y
Hierarchical differences reporting	Y	Y	Y	Y	Y	Y	Y	Y	Z	Y
Config control forms registers	Z	Z	Y	Y	Z	Y	Z	Z	Y	Z
Hierarchical CI and file layout	Z	Z	Y	Y	Z	N	Z	Z	Y	N

APPENDIX B
GLOSSARY OF TERMS AND LIST OF ABBREVIATIONS

Access control   The ability to allow and disallow access to any/all parts of the controlled area for such actions as 'submit', 'get-for-change', 'browse', 'release'. The access controls should be set up and modified by the configuration manager only, within the CM tool, as directed by the TRC.

Approval/Authorization   Signifies approval by TRC, CCB and/or the customer (whichever is applicable) for implementation of a change or any other action or sentence detailed in a configuration control form.

Archive   The *retrievable* removal of a file or record, from the controlled area (e.g. the off-lining of temporarily unwanted CIs to make space available).

As built state   The description of a baselined configuration (e.g. as it has been installed). See **Build state log**

Baseline   A specific reference point in the project's life cycle. Formal baselines (e.g. delivery) relate to project milestones, as defined in a project's quality plan; informal baselines (e.g. integration builds) will be established during the design and development phases of the project. Achievement of any baseline signifies clearance of all associated actions and conformance with the respective, *pre-defined* baseline criteria.

Baseline control   The control of an entire configuration which meets the criteria of a specific baseline or release. For example, a number of software modules in a configuration hierarchy may have been enhanced/corrected and the function of baseline control is to ensure that all the CIs—and only those CIs—earmarked for a specific baseline are included in it.

Build control/management   An automated facility for rebuilding software CIs where one or more files within a component have changed. Fully automated build control will ensure that only files which have been changed since the last build are recompiled.

Build state log   A complete list of all CIs and their software, hardware inventories and/or drawings files, that make up a particular configuration. Build state logs should detail not only the CI names and file names, but also their current issue or as built status, together with the dates they were submitted to or logged in the formal controlled area and references to any defects or enhancements impacting them.

Cancellation   Decision that no further action should be taken in progressing a configuration control form (e.g. due to withdrawal or rejection).

Change control   The process of impact assessment of proposed changes to CIs—whether resulting from problems/defects or requests for enhancement—and the controlled and verified implementation of approved changes.

CI submission form (or CI record)   A fixed-format configuration control form, used to identify new and updated CIs on their submission/re-submission to the controlled area. CISFs may be used to supply the data for the master configuration index.

CM library   See **Controlled area**

Component   Used in the context of this book to describe an identifiable part of a project. Software components may be made up of several modules, with each component itself forming part of the system whole. Formally controlled components are configuration items (CIs).

Concession   Permission granted by quality assurance and/or the customer to use or distribute a product, or one or more of a product's constituent parts, which does not comply with the specified technical requirements. Concessions may be minor (in-house) or major (customer).

Configuration   The functional and physical characteristics of a system, as described in technical documents and achieved in a product.

Configuration audit   The verification, by inspection, that established standards and procedures are implemented and followed by the project personnel responsible, and that the configuration described in status reports reflects that actually being tested/installed/used.

Configuration control   That part of configuration management which deals with the submission and withdrawal of the CIs in a formal controlled area (or CM library), the analysis of problems/defects associated with CIs in the controlled area, and the control of changes to the CIs.

Configuration controller   A member of the CM team, reporting to the configuration manager, who is responsible for the day-to-day maintenance of the formal controlled area structures, CIs, files and releases, the update and progression of control forms and the production of standard CM reports.

Configuration control form   A fixed-format, uniquely identifiable document, which gives details relating to configuration items and their status (e.g. change requests, submission forms, incident/defect reports, etc.).

Configuration control form status   Control forms have a *global* status of either 'Open' or 'Closed'. Within each global status, control forms will have a *progression* status that describes which part of the respective procedure is currently being followed. Examples of 'Open' progression status are 'Draft', 'For_Assessment', 'Implementing', etc. Examples of 'Closed' progression status are 'Closed_Approved', 'Closed_Cancelled', etc.

Configuration identification The application of a unique identifier (or short name) to every CI which forms, or will form, part of a project's configuration and the planning of a project's CM system, including naming conventions, structures, etc. Also the planning of each baseline and CI in terms of its contents and timescales, together with the unique numbering of every configuration control form associated with each CI. Configuration identification also establishes the position of a given CI in the project's configuration hierarchy, together with its relationship to other CIs in that structure.

Configuration item (CI) Any part of the development and/or deliverable system (whether software, hardware, firmware, drawings, inventories and/or documentation) that needs to be *independently* identified, stored, tested, reviewed, used, changed, delivered and/or maintained. CIs differ widely in complexity and may contain other CIs in a hierarchy.

Configuration management (CM) The engineering and administrative disciplines (which include configuration identification, control, status accounting and auditing) that ensure that *every part* of the project's configuration is identified, reliable, traceable and repeatable.

Configuration manager The CM team leader, whose responsibilities include the design, implementation and maintenance of the CM system, the integrity of the formal controlled area, the production or availability of status accounting reports and audit trails, together with release management of updated CIs for formal test and/or use. The configuration manager may be the point of contact with the customer and sub-contractor(s) for matters relating to CM.

Configuration management processor A formally controlled computer (or partition) on which is stored all CM information, together with the environment tools and facilities with which the configuration is created, developed, maintained and reported on.

Controlled area (or CM library) A formally controlled, electronic area for the deposit and withdrawal of *soft* copies (i.e. electronic) of CIs, whether software, documentation, drawings and/or inventories. The controlled area also holds *hard* copies of document CIs (i.e. paper), for lending purposes, and all configuration control forms, whether in soft and/or hard format.

Customization The ability for a user to adapt a packaged (CM) tool to handle bespoke functionality, without the necessity to alter the tool's source code. For example, the creation of a configuration control form with event triggers, using scripts, pop-up menus and/or tool-specific syntax.

Defect reporting The analysis of reported incidents or defects on CIs, and the decision as to what clearance action should be taken (if any), i.e. cancellation, change, creation of a new CI, or concession. See **Sentence**

Deletion The *irretrievable* removal of a file or record, from the controlled area. Unlike archiving, once deletion has occurred, true traceability is no longer possible.

Development configuration control The informally controlled storage, maintenance and/or building of items that are not yet considered suitable for formal configuration control. Procedures governing development control will be far less stringent than those for formal control.

Dry run testing The complete *dress rehearsal* of a formal test, using items from development configuration control, in preparation for the submission of those items to formal configuration control, as CIs. The procedure used for a dry run test will be the formal test procedure, albeit that the procedure may be at draft issue status.

Escrow The lodging of an item or items into the custody of a third party until a specified condition has been fulfilled. In IT terms, may be used for lodging source code with the National Computing Centre (NCC), as security against suppliers being unable to support their software in the future.

External change A proposed change (usually documented on a change request) that impacts an organization's deliverable CIs, i.e. has direct impact on the customer and/or user.

File The lowest element of a software, inventory or document configuration hierarchy, which may be a CI in its own right or be contained in a CI.

Fix See **Patch**

Formal configuration control See **Configuration control**

Freeze A snapshot of a CI or group of CIs (which may be at draft or formal issue status) that guarantees repeatability of the CI at a particular draft or issue.

Groupware Packaged software that allows the sharing of information between groups and individuals. Information and work packages can 'flow' from one user to the next, but the emphasis and power of the packages is on the sharing. See also **Workflow**

Hard copy A CI or part of a CI, a control form or a status accounting report, which is produced in paper format.

Implementation The incorporation of approved change(s) into a CI or collection of CIs. Implementation of a change request is deemed to have been completed once the updated and retested CI has been resubmitted to the controlled area and re-released/distributed.

Internal change A proposed change (usually documented on a change request) that impacts an organization's development CIs only, i.e. has no direct impact on the customer and/or user.

Issue The status specification of a CI for reference and control purposes, during its planning or development stages and/or at the time of its distribution, test, installation, build, use, etc. A CI is described as being at either 'Draft' or 'Formal Issue' status.

Known deficiency An acknowledged deviation from requirement, documented on an incident/defect report (or similar document), which will result in either a change request to correct it, or a concession.

Lodge See **Submission**

Major change Any alteration to a CI that has considerable impact on the system's form, fit, function, time and/or cost (e.g. requirement specification enhancements).

Master configuration index (MCI) A list of all deliverable and non-deliverable CIs (usually sorted into CI type), documenting each CI's title, mnemonic and issue status.

Minor change Any alteration to a CI that does not affect the system's form, fit, function, time or cost (e.g. the addition of a new user account on a development operating system).

Moderate change Any alteration to a CI that impacts the system's form, fit, function, time and/or cost, but without undue escalation of timescales and/or manpower (e.g. re-design of an existing module).

Node The point of a plant stem from which leaves arise. In the context of a system specification tree (SST), the point of a configuration structure from which CIs or further CI structures arise. Nodes may be actual CIs (e.g. 'Module_D'), sub-CIs (e.g. sub-directories) or descriptive 'hooks' for categorizing CIs (e.g. 'Source_code').

Non-conformance A deviation from a specification or other technical requirement. Non-conforming material should be documented on incident/defect reports (or similar documents) and subsequently either corrected or conceded.

Owner The member of project or sub-contractor staff who is allocated responsibility for the production of a CI and/or its maintenance. The owner of a CI is documented as the 'Originator' on the CI's submission form.

Patch The inclusion of a temporary software file(s) in a copy of a software CI, or the temporary alteration in a hardware configuration, which is found to be defective. Patching enables testing or use to continue where it would otherwise be unwise or impossible to do so. All patches must be fully documented on incident/defect reports (or similar document) and *totally overwritten/reconfigured* by subsequent, clearance submissions and installations of the respective CI(s).

Recommendation Signifies agreement with configuration control form details and recommendation to proceed to the next step in the control form procedure.

Register A fixed-format report giving details of specific configuration control forms and/or the CIs affected/described by them (e.g. a register of 'Open' CRs).

Rejection Refusal to recommend that a configuration control form proceed to the next step in the respective procedure, or refusal by TRC, CCB and/or the customer to approve a decision, action or sentence detailed in a configuration control form (e.g. rejection of a change request would result in either its rework or cancellation).

Release/distribution The act of making CIs available to other members of the project and/or the customer, for review, test, integration, use, etc.

Reliabiity Proof that an item will react in an identical manner when put through identical tests in an identical environment. Thus a CI may be deemed to be 'reliable' even if a known deficiency has been flagged against it, on the condition that the deficiency is repeatable in a controlled environment.

Repeatability   The ability to reproduce a CI, baseline or total configuration exactly as it was at a given point in time or in a given release. Repeatability also ensures that it is possible to verify that the reproduction has been correctly implemented.

Restore   Reinstalling a file or record in the controlled area which has previously been archived (e.g. following the off-lining of temporarily unwanted CIs to make space available).

Sentence   The decision taken (by an objective technical authority such as a TRC chairman and/or QA) as to what should happen to an incident/defect report, e.g. 'Cancel', 'Raise a Change Request', 'Concede', etc.

Soft copy   A CI or part of a CI, a control form or a status accounting report, which is produced in *electronic*, not paper, format.

Status accounting   The mechanism for gathering information/data (metrics) on CIs and their control forms, together with the production and analysis of reports on that information/data (measurement).

Structure(s)   The definition of the hierarchical dependency and interrelationships between CIs in a configuration (e.g. a set of directories and sub-directories).

Submission   The electronic deposit of soft CI files in the controlled area (or references to those files, if they are held on some form of transfer medium, e.g. disc), and/or the lodging of hard copy documentation, hardware inventories and/or drawings for formal configuration control, together with the recording of that deposit and any information affecting it.

System environment   The hardware and software (both proprietary and bespoke) environment on which a project's CIs are developed, tested, built and/or used and the relevant issue status of each part of that environment (e.g. the operating system, compiler, processor make, model and serial number, printers, plotters, etc.).

System specification tree (SST)   The graphic representation, in a tree root structure, of the overall relationship between CIs throughout the evolution of design. The first CI is the total system and is represented by the top of the tree. As system design proceeds, the project breaks into further high-level CIs that are themselves defined by yet further specifications. As the project passes through the design and development phases, an increasing complexity of CI specifications defines the project in ever greater detail. For maintenance systems, the establishment of an SST often has to be achieved through reverse engineering.

Traceability   Part of configuration status accounting, whereby a complete history of any/all CIs is known and can be proven.

Version control   The allocation of a status number to every file and CI within the controlled area, and the incrementation of those numbers whenever a file or CI is changed. Version control also includes the ability to trace the differences between versions, and is closely linked with access control.

Workflow   Packaged software that proactively manages the flow of work between users, according to predefined rules (usually documented in a procedure). Workflow packages coordinate users and appropriate data resources, to achieve defined objectives by set deadlines.

LIST OF THE ABBREVIATIONS USED

ANSI	American National Standards Institute
AOB	Any Other Business
API	Application Programmer Interface
AQAP	Allied Quality Assurance Publication
AWOL	Absent Without Official Leave
BCS	British Computer Society
BS	British Standard
BSI	British Standards Institution
CASE	Computer-Aided System Engineering
CCB	Configuration Control Board
CCRB	Customer Configuration Review Board
CCTA	Central Computing & Telecommunications Agency
CESG	Communications-Electronics Security Group
CI	Configuration Item
CISF	Configuration Item Submission Form
CIWF	Configuration Item Withdrawal Form
CM	Configuration Management
CMDB	Configuration Management Database
CMF	Configuration Management Facility (TM)
CMM	Capability Maturity Model
CMS	Code Management System (TM)
CR	Change Request
CV	Curriculum Vitae
DAT	Data Transfer Tape
DEC	Digital Equipment company
DEF STAN	Defence Standard
DSS	Department of Social Security
ECN	Engineering Change Notification
ECP	Engineering Change Proposal
ECR	Engineering Change Request
EN	European (Standard)
5GL	Fifth-Generation Language
FPA	Function Point Analysis

GAK	Gemeenschappelijk Administratie Kantoor (i.e. the Dutch DSS)
GUI	Graphical User Interface
HCI	Human-Computer Interface
HDC	Help Desk Call
HMG	Her Majesty's Government
H/W	Hardware
IBM	International Business Machines
ID	Identifier
IDR	Incident/Defect Report
IEEE	Institute of Electrical & Electronic Engineers
IS	Information System(s)
ISM	(BCS) Industry Structure Model
ISO	International Organization for Standardization
IT	Information Technology
ITIL	IT Infrastructure Library
LAN	Local Area Network
LOC	Lines of Code
MCI	Master Configuration Index
MoD	Ministry of Defence
NASA	(USA) National Aeronautics and Space Administration
NATO	North Atlantic Treaty Organisation
OA	Office Automation
OHP	Overhead Projector
OR	Operational Requirement
PC	Portable Computer
PCC	Project Configuration Controller
PCMS	Process Configuration Management System (TM)
PVCS	Polytron Version Control System (TM)
QA	Quality Assurance
QAR	Quality Assurance Representative
QIP	Quality Improvement Process
QMS	Quality Management System
RCS	Revision Control System (TM)
RTS	Run-time System
SCCS	Source Code Control System (TM)
SEI	Software Engineering Institute
SLA	Service Level Agreement
SQC	Software Quality Control
SST	System Specification Tree
STANAG	(NATO) Standardisation Agreement

S/W	Software
T&A	Test and Acceptance
tbd	To be defined
TMF	Transfer Media Form
TRC	Technical Review Committee
WAN	Wide Area Network
WBS	Work Breakdown Structure

APPENDIX C
BIBLIOGRAPHY

Below are listed a number of titles that appear as a result of the author's reading experience and library searches on configuration management. It is very noticeable that, while there are several books which deal with the problem of software CM, none of the titles found covers the far wider issues of a total system.

What these books offer in terms of software CM is sound; there are good examples of procedures and configuration control forms that could be used on any project. With the exception of the CCTA ITIL Service Support Set and the collection of national and international standards, however, all the publications are aimed at engineers. While this backs up the statement that CM is a technical, not just administrative function, it shows that the myriad of interfaces to CM, from *all* sections of a project throughout *all* its phases, have not been described in full and, in particular, directorates, commercial management and customers have not yet been adequately targeted.

Ashley, N. and Measurement Team, *A Starter Kit for Setting Up a Measurement Programme*, Brameur Ltd, Fleet, 1994.

Babich, W.A., *Software Configuration Management—Coordination for Team Productivity*, Addison-Wesley, Wokingham, 1986.

Ben-Menachem, M., *Software Configuration Management Guidebook*, McGraw-Hill, Maidenhead, 1995.

Berlack, R., *Software Configuration Management*, Wiley, Chichester, 1991.

Bersoff, E.H., Henderson, V.D. and Siegel, S.G., *Software Configuration Management—An Investment in Product Integrity*, Prentice-Hall, London, 1980.

British Computer Society, Industry Structure Model (Release 2), BCS, London, 1991.

BSI, *BS EN ISO 9000* and *10000 Series*, British Standards Institution, 1980–1995.

BSI, *BS 6488 Configuration Management Standard*, British Standards Institution, 1984.

Buckle, J.K., *Software Configuration Management*, Macmillan, London, 1982.

CCTA, *ITIL Service Support Set—Change Management Module*, Central Computing & Telecommunications Agency, 1989.

CCTA, *ITIL Service Support Set—Configuration Management Module*, Central Computing & Telecommunications Agency, 1990.

CCTA, *ITIL Service Support Set—Problem Management Module*, Central Computing & Telecommunications Agency, 1990.

CCTA, *ITIL Service Support Set—Software Control & Distribution Module*, Central Computing & Telecommunications Agency, 1990.

CESG, *Computer Security Memorandum No. 7*, HMG Communications Headquarters, Communications-Electronics Security Group, UK, August 1990.

Goodman, P., *Practical Implementation of Software Metrics*, McGraw-Hill, Maidenhead, 1993.

IEEE, *ANSI/IEEE Std 828: Standard for Software Configuration Management Plans*, Institute of Electrical and Electronic Engineers, 1984/1990.

MoD, *DEF STAN 57-50/2: Configuration Management Policy and Procedures for Defence Material*, Ministry of Defence, UK, September 1985.

NATO, *AQAPs 1, 13* and *14*, North Atlantic Treaty Organisation, 1984.

Paulk, M.C., Curtis, B., Chrissis, M.B. and Weber, C.V., *Capability Maturity Model for Software, Version 1.1*. Software Engineering Institute, CMU/SEI-93-TR-24, Pittsburgh, Pa., February, 1993.

Whitgift, D., *Methods and Tools for Software Configuration Management*, Wiley, Chichester, 1991.

INDEX